# Frauds, Phones & Fingerprints

## Proving Your Identity in the Digital Age

Almis Ledas

FriesenPress

One Printers Way
Altona, MB R0G 0B0
Canada

www.friesenpress.com

ISBN
978-1-03-833333-9 (Hardcover)
978-1-03-833332-2 (Paperback)
978-1-03-833334-6 (eBook)

*1. COMPUTERS, INTERNET, SECURITY*

Distributed to the trade by The Ingram Book Company

Frauds, Phones & Fingerprints

# Table of Contents

Acknowledgements . . . . . . . . . . . . . . . . . . . . . . . . . . . . . . . . . . . . . . . . vii

Preface . . . . . . . . . . . . . . . . . . . . . . . . . . . . . . . . . . . . . . . . . . . . . . . . . . ix

Introduction . . . . . . . . . . . . . . . . . . . . . . . . . . . . . . . . . . . . . . . . . . . . . xiii

One: The Holy Trinity of Identity . . . . . . . . . . . . . . . . . . . . . . . . . . . . 1

Two: The Digital Challenge . . . . . . . . . . . . . . . . . . . . . . . . . . . . . . . . 15

Three: Your Credit Card Knows Who You Are . . . . . . . . . . . . . . 33

Four: Your Phone as Your Avatar . . . . . . . . . . . . . . . . . . . . . . . . . . . 45

Five: Is Social Media Killing Privacy? . . . . . . . . . . . . . . . . . . . . . . 61

Six: Big Brother is Watching . . . . . . . . . . . . . . . . . . . . . . . . . . . . . . 75

Seven: Saved by a Treefort . . . . . . . . . . . . . . . . . . . . . . . . . . . . . . . 89

Eight: The SecureKey Solution . . . . . . . . . . . . . . . . . . . . . . . . . . . . 97

Nine: Bluink and the Identity Wallet . . . . . . . . . . . . . . . . . . . . . 111

Ten: The Problem is Choice . . . . . . . . . . . . . . . . . . . . . . . . . . . . . . 119

Eleven: The Road Ahead . . . . . . . . . . . . . . . . . . . . . . . . . . . . . . . . 129

Conclusion . . . . . . . . . . . . . . . . . . . . . . . . . . . . . . . . . . . . . . . . . . . . 141

Endnotes . . . . . . . . . . . . . . . . . . . . . . . . . . . . . . . . . . . . . . . . . . . . . 145

References . . . . . . . . . . . . . . . . . . . . . . . . . . . . . . . . . . . . . . . . . . . . 153

# Acknowledgements

The identity verification industry, especially in Canada, is a close-knit community. I would like to acknowledge the help and input from its members, sometimes referred to as the "identirati," especially those who contributed directly with ideas, input and interviews, including Robert Blumenthal, Steve Borza, Jay and Kim Krushell, Brian McCabe, Pierre Roberge, Greg Wolfond and Yiping Yi.

Jonathan Blackburn made invaluable contributions to the readability of this work. I met him over twenty years ago in a running club in Toronto where we ran every Sunday for the better part of a decade, running both New York and Boston marathons as well. When we reconnected many years later for a run, I learned he had become a capable editor, and he kindly agreed to edit this work. The elegance you find in the prose owes much to him.

FriesenPress did more than make the publication of this book possible. Their editors helped me find my voice and ensured that my language was not overly burdened with the industry jargon that invariably creeps into business writing. Their capable staff also guided me through every step of the journey to the publication of the book you hold in your hands.

Finally, I thank my family. In completing her doctorate, Adri van Hilten, my lovely and academically gifted wife, showed me new possibilities and inspired me to undertake this effort. My adventurous daughter, Alexandra, keeps me grounded, shows me how much there still is to learn and gives me hope for the future.

# Preface

There are many books out there on the subject of identity in the digital age. That's because identity, especially in its digital context, is complex and multifaceted. You can look at digital identity from many different angles. It can be explored from a legal perspective – the legislation governing identity, even the distinction between identity theft and identity fraud, has attracted attention from academics. You can look at the technology of identity verification, which offers many areas of study, such as cryptography, biometrics and blockchains, any one of which could fill volumes. There are books that deal with identity from the perspective of security, privacy and the protection of personal information. These topics, and others, are usually tackled by specialists providing insight to other specialists or advocating for a solution to a challenge yet to be fully solved, and they're usually dense in terminology and jargon. It can make them impenetrable to the casual reader.

So why read another one? Because I could find no book that was able to explain the challenges of identity in the digital world in plain language to a reader new to the subject. And that is what you now have before you.

My background is in engineering and technology, but I'm a generalist rather than a specialist. I've heard that a specialist is someone who knows more and more about less and less, until they know everything about nothing. I suffer from the opposite affliction.

It was through luck rather than foresight that I joined the wireless industry in its early days. For over three decades, I had the good fortune to help it grow to maturity in the company of the talented business and technical leaders who were creating the global marvel that wireless has become. I had a front-row seat to the cell phone's transformation from a cumbersome business tool to a consumer status symbol, to a common personal communicator and to the revolutionary multipurpose device it is today. In the process, I gained an appreciation for the ways in which technology and human behaviour shape one another, often in unanticipated ways.

I spent the final decade of my career working with Canada's three national wireless telecommunications companies, called telcos, leading a company that was delivering identity verification solutions. It was this experience that convinced me there were many digital identity stories worth telling. Identity and its verification was not well understood, and it didn't receive much attention from technology's business leaders. They were focused on delivering the best possible customer experience and reducing costs. At the same time, consumers were seeking convenience, often at the expense of security. The identity challenge began attracting a new breed of entrepreneur looking for ways to enhance security without compromising convenience or cost.

As if delivering convenience, low cost and security was not enough of a challenge, there was even more to consider. A governing authority that could effectively ensure the security of one's digital identity would have enough access to personal information to be seen as a privacy concern. This alone could prevent people from using it.

Combine technology, human behaviour, business challenges and creative entrepreneurs, add in concerns over government oversight and personal privacy, spice it up with stories of world-class fraud and cybercrime, and you get the story of digital identity that I would like to tell.

# Introduction

> All of us take pride and pleasure in the fact that we are unique, but I'm afraid that when all is said and done the police are right: it all comes down to fingerprints.
>
> David Sedaris, *Holidays on Ice*

THE FBI DEFINES IDENTITY THEFT as the stealing and using of personal information, like a name or social security number, to commit fraud. In one striking example, Demi Moore, once Hollywood's highest paid actress, was the victim of identity theft perpetrated by David Matthew Read and Marc Ian Higley. Posing as Demi Moore's personal assistant, Read reported her "no limit" American Express Black Card stolen and requested a replacement, which he and Higley were able to pick up at a Federal Express depot in Santa Monica, California, using forged identification. The thieves then purchased $169,000 worth of merchandise at Nordstrom, Apple, Bloomingdale's and Saks Fifth Avenue at locations in and around Los Angeles, before stashing the goods in a storage locker, with plans to later resell them. The fraudsters were identified and apprehended, thanks to store security systems that captured them on camera and Read's use of his personal debit card at one of the stores. Assisting in the identification was the fact that Read was already known to the Glendale Police Department for allegedly buying a Mercedes using another victim's identity.[1]

You might think that convincingly masquerading as a celebrity would be risky for a fraudster, but Tiger Woods, Ricky Gervais, Liv Tyler and Will Smith have all been similarly victimized.[2] According to the FBI's *2021 Internet Crime Report*, documented cases of identity theft in the United States more than tripled in two years, reaching 51,629 with losses of $278 million in 2021. Boston-based consultancy Aite-Novarica reported that 47 percent of Americans experienced identity theft leading to a financial loss in 2020.

The financial impact of identity theft is not the only cause for concern. Criminals have been known to provide law enforcement with personal information other than their own, causing unsuspecting people to receive court summonses or bench warrants for their arrest. Stolen medical information has enabled fraudsters to receive care using another person's insurance. This can deny the fraud victim treatment if fraudulent claims have maxed out their policy's limits. More dangerously, should the victim require emergency care, their medical file may be compromised by documentation of procedures they didn't receive, causing misdiagnosis by medical professionals. Stolen identity information is also being used to create synthetic identities used for multiple types of criminal activity related to insurance, land transfer and money laundering.

What has driven this wave of identity theft in the new millennium? History shows us that the regulation of transactions has always prioritized maintaining the integrity of commercial systems over protecting individual victims. When fraud did occur, regulations focused on determining which of the parties involved would, or should, have had the best opportunity to detect that the actors were not who they claimed to be and then allocating losses.

Digitization has accelerated the pace of transactions, but our tools for verifying identity have not kept up.

Transacting remotely – online or over the phone – has undermined the effectiveness of established methods of identity verification, forcing reliance on only the truth of the information provided for proof of identity. Information is more easily copied, transmitted and (increasingly) stolen than a physical credential. Copied information is indistinguishable from the original source material. Any time goods or money are exchanged for a promise of future performance, there's an incentive for the fraudster to make off with the goods, leaving fulfilment of that promise to someone else. Cases of stolen credit card information are common, but stolen personal information has let fraudsters drive off with new cars, leaving the loan obligations to unsuspecting others, or make off with the proceeds from the sale of property that belonged to someone else. Stolen account information has let fraudsters make unauthorized transfers of funds from accounts and steal millions in cryptocurrency. Database breaches, phishing and unprotected exchanges of information have made personally identifiable information (PII) readily obtainable by those so inclined to find it. With PII forming the basis of much digital identity verification, identity theft has never been easier, leading to unprecedented levels of financial crime. According to the UK-based International Compliance Association, financial crime accounts for 3.6 percent of the global gross domestic product (GDP). If financial crime were a country, it would be the fifth-largest economy in the world.

Identity verification in the digital world has proven to be a significant challenge – in part, because the methods we use to establish identity in the real world rely on human judgement. Evolution has given each of us the ability to recognize people we know. When we encounter people we don't know, we have to rely on the presentation of identity-bearing credentials issued by reliable authorities. If you're carrying John Smith's passport and you look like the passport photo, you are probably John Smith. We accept this, despite the fact that the passport was originally created to be a travel document, not a means of identity verification. With no reliable template for bringing identity into the digital world, different methods for adding security have emerged. While these have led to new business opportunities in digital identity verification, there's been no widespread adoption of an effective or standardized solution. In the meantime, businesses and governments, attracted by the efficiency of digital channels, are digitizing client interactions – opening the door to identity theft and cybercrime.

Identity verification in the digital world is further complicated by human nature: we rely heavily on intuition for making day-to-day decisions. We know to lock the door when we leave the house, we have learned how to protect our valuables and we know how to safely navigate the streets. Evolution has prepared us to respond to immediate threats, but we are notoriously poor at judging the likelihood of remote future hazards. Not only is our judgement influenced by recent events and news stories (what psychologists call "recency bias"), but we resist making the analytical effort to rationally understand and assess risk. Add in the fact that both digital identity verification and online privacy are poorly understood, and we have fertile ground for fraudsters. We favour convenience over security. We adopt online practices without fully understanding their implications. We rely on digital security tools without understanding how they work and their limitations.

For most of human history, privacy was taken for granted, and surveillance required sophisticated effort. In the digital age, gathering information on people is no longer a difficult task, making privacy a legitimate concern. Some measures being taken to preserve personal privacy have even come to stand in the way of stronger digital identity verification.

In this book, we'll explore how to know whether people are who they say they are, both in the real world and the digital one.

We'll better understand how people know who we are when we interact online, and the ways someone might impersonate us. Methods to verify identity in the real world are well established, but fraud still occurs. Sometimes this is because we sacrifice security in the interest of convenience; other times, it's because a resourceful fraudster has discovered a way to exploit a weakness in the verification process. The same challenges exist in the digital world, except that fraudsters have more opportunities. Digital identity credentials are easier to steal and easier to copy; fraudsters can execute multiple attacks and take advantage of statistical probabilities that we don't see or appreciate.

In many cases, fraudsters don't have to be particularly resourceful to exploit the system, and exploit it they do. In response, both entrepreneurs and major technology companies have stepped up with longer passwords, password keepers, biometrics, multifactor authentication and document scanning, but no comprehensive solution to the problem is yet in sight. There are promising tools for identity verification being developed for the digital world, some of which already give us an appreciation for what the future will hold. Tools, however, will not be enough to eliminate the scourge of identity theft unless we also learn how to protect personal information and assess online threats. Even as we do so, there will, no doubt, be more surprises still to come.

# 1 The Holy Trinity of Identity

Identity is a uniquely human concept. It is that ineffable "I" of self-consciousness, something that is understood worldwide by every person living in every culture. As René Descartes said, *Cogito ergo sum* – I think, therefore I am.

Christopher Allen,
"The Path to Self-Sovereign Identity"

THE WORD "IDENTITY" IS FAMILIAR, yet it can be hard to define. Like liberty, privacy or security, identity depends on the context in which it's used. While there can be existential and aspirational aspects to identity, in its most basic form, it aims to address the question "Who are you as a unique individual?" The answer to the question usually consists of a name combined with personal information distinguishing you from others. When there's doubt, a credible third party is called upon to authenticate the answer.

Three methods are used to authenticate identity, and they're commonly known as "something you are," "something you have" and "something you know." Being recognized by someone who knows you is the most basic example of "something you are" – your physical presence itself can be used to identify you. But "something you are" can also be your fingerprints, your voice, a retinal scan or any other biometric that can be matched against a known record for verification. "Something you have" is the authentication method we use most often when we're confronted by someone we don't know. This can be an employee card or access pass, a driver's licence, a passport or even a key that opens a lock. An example of "something you know" is the combination of a username and password for accessing a website, but it can also be the combination to a lock, a passcode or the answer to a knowledge-based question to verify identity for a call centre. These three methods of identity verification are well established in the real world. Attempts to adapt them to the digital world have met with mixed success.

## Something You Are

Understanding people as unique individuals comes naturally to us. A human baby will recognize its parents with no instruction. It's something even our pets can do: distinguishing their owners from strangers. This ability is not learned by individuals; it's learned through evolution. We are accustomed to using our instincts to recognize people, sometimes pausing to search our memories, but we seldom rely on a rigorous analytical process. Our brains keep a record of people we've known and match that record to them when we see these people again. Some people are better at this than others, but the process usually occurs without conscious effort. It's instinctive and automatic.

In his 2011 book, *Thinking, Fast and Slow*, psychologist Daniel Kahneman defined two modes of thought called system 1 and system 2. System 1 is fast, instinctive and emotional; system 2 is slow, deliberate and logical, requiring effort. System 1 governs breathing, eating and survival; over time, it also takes over learned skills, such as reading and reaction to social impulses. System 2 runs at a low level of engagement until called upon. If presented with a problem in mathematics that we're unlikely to solve instinctively, we call upon system 2 to solve it analytically. Similarly, if system 1 stimulates anger, system 2 may be called upon to modulate our behaviour to enable a polite response.

For most of human history, our understanding of identity was managed exclusively by system 1. People were either known and immediately recognized, or unknown and then assessed based on appearance and intuition. Seldom was a logical, analytical process for determining the identity of a person required. On the occasions it was needed, it was cumbersome and inefficient. After an army led by Burgundian Duke Charles the Bold was defeated by René II, Duke of Lorraine, at the battle of Nancy in 1477, the battlefield was looted for hours. The vanquished Charles the Bold, now naked and frozen, was left unrecognizable. It took four days for his closest associates – his Italian page, his physician, his half-brother and chronicler Olivier de la Marche – to identify him by means of distinctive signs on his body.[3] Only when the body had been washed and clothed was he recognized by his courtiers.

Since identifying a person is an instinctive, automatic process, it's hard to pass the ability on to someone else. This was especially true before we could create reliable images of people. If a person were described as tall or short, thin or stocky, with specified hair colour or additional features, the result remained open to interpretation. This explains why early "Wanted" posters described criminals by their apparel, making no mention of age, height or facial features. Fifteenth century legal sources contain many examples of such detailed descriptions – the gray patched coats and black hats of two alleged Hussite arsonists, or the blue stockings of a card trickster sought in Erfurt in 1412.[4]

It wasn't until the nineteenth century that the first attempt at systematic personal description to assist with identity verification occurred. Because law enforcement could not verify the identity of apprehended criminals, hardened criminals were frequently being sentenced as first offenders. To solve this problem, French ethnologist Alphonse Bertillon introduced a system of classification in which measurements of body parts, together with eye colour and hair colour, allowed a person to be categorized into one of 1,701 separate groupings, which helped to identify repeat offenders.

Bertillon's system used index cards to store photographs of criminals and their personal characteristics, such as foot length, skull width, ear shape and length of left middle finger. The dimensions enabled classification into one of 243 categories, which when combined with seven different combinations of hair and eye colour, created 1,701 different categories in total. Once a person had been categorized, their photograph would be used to match them to an existing record in that category. This system was adopted by the Paris Police in 1882. Its success led to its adoption throughout Europe, and by 1887, it was implemented in the United States in Illinois.

At the same time as the Bertillon system was being adopted, Sir Francis Galton, a cousin of Charles Darwin, was using fingerprints in his study of the characteristics of heredity. He learned that a person's fingerprints remained consistent throughout their life and came to believe that no two fingerprints were alike. In his book *Finger Prints*, published in 1892, he wrote:

> Let no one despise the ridges on account of their smallness, for they are in some respects the most important of all anthropological data. We shall see that they form patterns, considerable in size and of a curious variety of shape, whose boundaries can be firmly outlined, and which are little worlds in themselves. They have the unique merit of retaining all their peculiarities unchanged throughout life, and afford in consequence an incomparably surer criterion of identity than any other bodily feature.[5]

Building on Bertillon's system and using "modern processes of photographic printing" to enlarge the images made of fingerprints, Galton identified the three most common fingerprint types – loop, whorl and arch – and created a system for fingerprint classification. The field was advanced by a number of contributors, but it was Sir Edward Richard Henry, commissioner of the London Metropolitan Police from 1903 to 1918, who is credited with the Henry Classification System of 1,024 fingerprint types, which was adopted by Scotland Yard to create a Central Fingerprint Bureau. In the United States, the New York Police Department, the New York State Prison System and the Federal Bureau of Prisons began using a fingerprint identification system in 1903, followed by the US Army in 1905.

Word of Galton's findings must have spread quickly, since a police official in Argentina is reported to have used Galton's research to create a fingerprint system that helped solve a murder in 1892 by way of a thumbprint.[6] In the United States, the first murder case to be successfully prosecuted using fingerprint evidence was the *People v. Jennings*, in which Thomas Jennings was convicted of the murder of Clarence Hiller (and subsequently hanged) based on fingerprints found at Hiller's house, establishing fingerprint evidence as reliable in a court of law.

Fingerprints replaced the Bertillon system in law enforcement, going on to become the primary means of verifying identity in the twentieth century; they are still used for identification today. The FBI automated its fingerprint card system in 1991 and linked it to other law enforcement systems to create the Integrated Automated Fingerprint Identification System in 1999. The system can deliver fingerprints to law enforcement officers in under two hours.

The computer-assisted data storage and matching capabilities that enhanced the power of fingerprint analytics have also been applied to other biometrics. Eye vein imaging and facial recognition were commercially implemented in the late 1990s, and advances in analytical tools and processing power have expanded biometric verification to include voice recognition, gait recognition, heart rate analysis and DNA.

Our innate, instinctive ability to recognize people we know, by matching images against stored memories, is being replicated in automated systems using a wide range of analytical tools. There appears to be no limit to the expanding range of ways to define "something you are" so long as there's access to a physical being.

## Something You Have

Today, each of us has a set of identification credentials. The average wallet contains a few credit cards, one or more bank cards, a driver's licence, a health card, perhaps a birth certificate, an assortment of loyalty cards, club cards, an employee pass, a gym membership, a transit pass, professional credentials, and maybe more. Many of these credentials are easily recognized by a layperson, who can judge their validity. Some time ago, however, this was not the case. Before the establishment of state infrastructure and formal addresses, people had no credentials. Originally, this presented few problems, as people were known to those around them. Problems started to arise when travel enabled passage from one state to another, introducing people to each other for the first time. How did people present themselves, and how were legitimate claims distinguished from those of imposters?

Valentin Groebner, a professor of medieval and Renaissance history at the University of Lucerne, has studied identity in the Middle Ages and documented numerous cases of impersonation. In 1515, the Swiss received a courier who delivered an urgent demand for more troops for a military campaign being waged in Italy. Unbeknownst to him, a properly credentialed courier had arrived a day earlier with the news that the campaign had been successfully concluded and the soldiers should be making their way home again. Some impersonations, like this one, were politically motivated, but others were carried out to collect the fees, gifts and meals customarily granted to those delivering messages. A false messenger turned up at the city council of Solothurn in 1495 claiming that King Maximilian had conquered Basel and was planning to attack the town. He was rewarded with a good meal and fifteen schillings, although it was later discovered that the town was in no danger.[7]

These first attempts to help solve the problem of impersonation were of the "something you have" variety. Official representatives were issued with credentials, badges or uniforms to identify them. More common for individuals, including some officials, were letters of introduction, which served to verify identity. These letters evolved into an early form of the passport, as they were used to grant safe passage to diplomats, couriers, merchants and pilgrims. For frequent travellers, like pilgrims, wearing a "pilgrim badge" – in addition to carrying a letter from their priest – provided added security, since the border guards they'd encounter were unlikely to be able to read.

Badges and letters were far from foolproof. Soon after their debut, reports of stolen badges and forged letters of introduction were common, and the false messenger became a stock figure in the literature of the fifteenth and sixteenth centuries.[8] With no way to create images of sufficient quality to permit identity verification, stolen letters and badges could be used by whoever had them in their possession. Craftsmen could create forged documents and badges that were indistinguishable from the originals. Issuing authorities began updating documents at regular intervals to control forgeries, but this was far from effective.

Documentation of any kind was rarely available to those beyond the privileged few who were able to travel or those in special circumstances, such as soldiers on leave in France, who were required, by royal decree, to carry a pass explaining their absence from their regiment. The common citizen, however, was unlikely to either need or carry identification.

Does this mean that there were no records of any kind? We know that documenting the population dates back to biblical times, when authorities kept records for tax collection and for drafting eligible men into the military. In many countries, the church also kept records of births, marriages and deaths. However, in "The Identification of the Citizen," French historian Gérard Noiriel reports that civil registration was viewed by the church as secondary to a religious ritual. Records were, at best, uneven, with people identified by name, but place and date of birth rarely captured. Different churches maintained records in different forms, making it tricky to authenticate any record provided. In France, registration only applied to Catholics; Protestants were excluded until 1685, and Jews had no civil status. Even when a birth was properly recorded, the record remained in the church, as there was no such thing as a birth certificate. With the passage of time, this meant there was no way to link an individual back to a birth record. Often people did not keep track of their own birth and would have only a vague notion of their own age. In Corsica in 1820, of 1,699 men registered for military service, 687 had no date of birth recorded. Others were able to avoid military service using false claims of marriage. This situation with public records persisted across most countries into the modern era.

The introduction of child labour laws created the need for a verifiable age. In, "'Age Ought to Be a Fact': The Campaign against Child Labor and the Rise of the Birth Certificate," historian Susan J. Pearson recounts how, in 1898, twenty years after the passage of child labour laws in the state of Wisconsin, authorities were forced to rely on parents to provide the ages of their children. But parents lied and changed the records of their children's births in family bibles. The issue was troubling for child labour reformers, but it was also becoming a concern for advocates of compulsory schooling, juvenile courts and any other regulation that used age to define rights or obligations. In 1888, Connecticut school board official John Jennings complained, "It is almost impossible to secure definite information as to the ages of many of the children … in too many instances the age of the children is merely a matter of speculation with the parents; they preserve no record, and their memory on the subject is worthless."[9]

In the early twentieth century, between one-half and three-quarters of births in the United States were unregistered.[10] From 1900 to 1940, child labour reformers lobbied all levels of government to issue professionally produced documents that made a person's age and identity an objective fact. While a few forms of documentary birth evidence were considered, authorities came to depend on the birth certificate, and issuing birth certificates started to become a common practice.

It would take decades for the birth certificate to be common-place. Stories of underage volunteers joining the services in the Second World War are common; the American Veterans Center reported that over 200,000 underage volunteers served honourably during the war. Today, this seems hard to believe, but in the 1940s, being without a birth certificate was not unusual. The candidate was expected to attest to their age. When the federal government asked that workers in defence industries provide proof of citizenship, authorities around the country were inundated with requests for delayed registrations of birth.[11]

Another identity credential we have today is the passport. This distant relative of the letters permitting merchants and pilgrims to travel owes its reinvention to the League of Nations in the aftermath of the First World War. As the victorious Allies were redrawing national borders while negotiating the Treaty of Versailles, millions of refugees sought resettlement rather than face purges awaiting them back home. These included stranded prisoners, Russians who had fled Bolshevik rule, and Greeks,

Assyrians, Turks and Armenians fleeing hostile regimes. The chairman of Norway's League of Nations Association, Fridtjof Nansen, was tasked with crafting a solution to this problem. He created a document that would allow refugees to cross borders in a controlled manner and remain in a country for work, which came to be known as the Nansen passport. League of Nations passport conferences in 1920 and 1926 helped establish the passport as the document we know today, containing name, citizenship, primary physical data, history of previous travel, photograph, and descriptors such as gender and occupation.

As in many nations, in Britain, Canada and the United States, the passport is a document granted to a named individual by the state requesting safe conduct and conferring protection. The individual does not own the passport and is obligated to surrender it on demand. Because it is a credential granted by a trusted authority to a named individual, and because it has information that can be used to confirm the identity of the individual, it has become a trusted identity credential. The passport is generally considered to be a reliable document, but there are forged and counterfeit passports in circulation. In 1998, Anselim Udezue toured Austria, Germany and Switzerland for nine months using tourist visas for each of these countries that he had applied for with his British Honduras passport. As he was leaving Switzerland, an airport official noticed that there was no such country as the British Honduras.[12]

In terms of safeguards against misuse, no personal credential has improved its security as quickly and consistently as the credit card. The microprocessor-enabled, radio frequency identification–equipped credit card of today would be unrecognizable to those who introduced the cardboard Diners Club card in 1950. From its inception, identity was vital to the credit card – a credit card gave access to immediate services and purchases, shifting the responsibility for future payment to the person named on the card.

In the hands of someone other than the legitimate card holder, it's a licence to steal.

Soon after the Bank of America mailed its first active credit cards to 60,000 clients in 1958, cases of credit card fraud began to be reported. With account information openly visible on a card, it could be used by anyone who could steal or duplicate it – and moving information to a magnetic stripe in the 1960s was a technical enhancement to which fraudsters also quickly adapted. It was not until the introduction of cards equipped with microprocessors and personal identification numbers (PINs) in the 1980s that card security got ahead of the fraudsters. These cards required specialized terminals for retailers to process transactions. In the 1990s, the card-processing associations developed standards for how the systems would work together, and in the early 2000s, standardized cards and terminals spread throughout retailers across the globe. Highly secure chip and PIN cards have now virtually eliminated credit card fraud at physical points of retail. This, however, has redirected the efforts of fraudsters online, resulting in over half of all Americans now having reported fraudulent charges on their accounts. This is but one example of how the effectiveness of "something you have" in the real world does not translate into the digital one.

## Something You Know

In the story of Ali Baba and the forty thieves, the words, "Open, Sesame!" open a concealed door to a cave of treasures. "Something you know," in the form of words or phrases, appears as an identifier in the Bible and was reportedly used by Roman legions. For "something you know" to confirm identity, the relying party must either have assigned a password or be in possession of information that only the authorized individual would know. As with other forms of identity verification, the individual is asked to present something (in this case, information) that the relying party can then match against information on record. This can be a combination, the answer to a question or a password.

The first reported use of a password for computer access was in 1961 by MIT computer science professor Fernando Corbató. Since the computer interface did not lend itself to keys or biometrics, Professor Corbató assigned each computer user a unique password. The password remains the most common method for accessing computer hardware, software or applications, with many of us now managing scores, if not hundreds, of unique passwords.

The password was never chosen for its strength as an authenticator; it was chosen because it's easy to use. Asking for credentials in a war zone is more secure, but letting intruders get close enough to present credentials is hazardous. The password solves this problem. It's easy to implement, easy to manage and easy to test. On the flip side, it's easy to steal and can sometimes be easy to guess.

Another example of "something you know" in the real world is the combination lock. But a combination lock can be cracked through trial and error. A combination lock with three dials, each numbered zero to nine, will have a thousand different combinations; a person could exhaust the possibilities in an hour or two, and a computer can do it much faster.

In the digital world, there is (so far) no easy way to use "something you are" or "something you have" over a single channel of communication. Meeting their criteria appears to be achievable using a remote camera, but this can be misleading. The relying party – the entity that authenticates a user's identity and grants access to resources based on that identity – can ask for a still or live image to evaluate, but it can't be sure if the image provided is authentic in real-time or a digital fabrication. The relying party receives only a digital stream of information that could have been captured, stored or redirected.

"What you know," in the form of username and password, was enhanced by adding knowledge-based questions. If you forgot your password, you could identify yourself by providing previously recorded information, such as the name of your first pet or the high school you attended. But much of this is information can be researched, captured, stored and misused in the wrong hands.

"Password hygiene" – creating and effectively managing strong passwords – remains a challenge, with half the population admitting they rely on memory to manage passwords and reuse them across different applications. In 2023, the most commonly used password in the world was "123456"; the fourth-most common password was "password."[13]

## Identity Verification in Practice

Whether it's "something you are," "something you have" or "something you know," the basic method for establishing identity in the real world is the same. When dealing with someone we know, we compare what we see with what we expect. If we recognize it, and it seems authentic, we accept the identity.

When dealing with an unfamiliar person for the first time, we ask for an authentic credential that can be matched with one stored at a credible authority. This can be a driver's licence, a birth certificate, a passport or another document we know and trust. If the credential is accepted as authentic, the associated identity is accepted. If the identity is used to open an account with an organization, future encounters can be simplified if the organization assigns a new unique identifier – username, card, number or password – which would then be presented as proof going forward.

# 2 The Digital Challenge

Why is it so hard to create an identity layer for the Internet? Mainly because there is little agreement on what it should be and how it should be run.

Kim Cameron, "The Laws of Identity"

THE US FEDERAL TRADE COMMISSION reported that within a single six-month period between October 2020 and March 2021, almost 7,000 people lost, in total, more than $80 million in cryptocurrency to digital theft.[14] The losses occurred due to fake currency exchanges, phony investment sites and outright theft through the use of stolen identity credentials.

Stolen credentials used to log in to an account are the most common form of identity theft. Many online accounts are still secured by only a username and password, and although additional layers of security are becoming more common – and in some markets, required – fraudsters have developed ingenious ways of getting their hands on login credentials.

Phishing is the attempt to trick a person into providing their username and password. The most common attacks use a fraudulent message containing a link to a site requiring credentials to be entered. This could look like a message from your bank requesting that you log in to verify or reverse a suspicious transaction, or a message from your tax authority requiring you to log in to your bank to accept a tax refund. More creative attempts may tell you that your email password has expired, asking that you to log in to the server to reset it, only to be redirected to a site that harvests your username and password. Fraudulent messages from shopping sites will alert you of a suspicious transaction and ask you to cancel it. In all cases, the suspect is asked to provide login credentials that the fraudster then steals. Whatever action is performed at the fraudulent site is meaningless, serving only to avoid arousing suspicion that could prompt the individual to reset their password. Once credentials are in the fraudster's possession, they can access the funds and transfer them to new accounts, which are then swiftly emptied.

If the fraudster has compromised an individual's email account, the fraudster can use the individual's username to request a password reset for a financial account. Some password resets don't require re-authentication or rely only on knowledge-based questions for which answers can be found on social media sites. When a new password or reset link is emailed, the fraudster uses it to take control of the account.

Some fraudsters will collect personal information and open a bank account in an unsuspecting individual's name. The victim may have a good credit rating and be eligible for credit cards and loans that the fraudster can exploit. There have been examples where a forged driver's licence was all it took for the fraudster to take possession of a new car, leaving the victim with the car loan.

Finally, some financial fraud relies on entirely fictitious, or "synthetic," identity; here, the fraudster will build a profile associated with a name that they created by first opening a utility account or subscription service, leading to a file being opened with a credit bureau. After a credit history has been established, an application will be made for a bank account or credit card. Synthetic accounts can then be used to assist in other transactions or carry out money laundering.

## Digital Identity

The internet has been famously designed to preserve anonymity. Early users were known by internet protocol (IP) addresses or domain names issued by centralized authorities, and identified themselves by their email addresses, which, in turn, led them to become dependent on suppliers for their online identities. For security, service providers would request a password to verify identity; having each relationship independently verified caused people to manage a large number of passwords. Websites imposed different requirements for passwords, specifying length or character combinations, to prevent password reuse and enhance security. People had to choose between reusing a small number of passwords, which compromised security, and managing a large number of unique passwords, which compromised convenience. Most people chose convenience over security.

Problems with online security soon became apparent, but solutions were elusive. Early attempts to reuse login credentials or create a federated identity, a single sign-on that allows you to move across systems without having to log in again, such as "sign in with Facebook," were met with skepticism. While using a single authentication token reduced the number of passwords people needed to remember, it moved identity management to a new centralized authority, in this case, Facebook. People were uncomfortable with running their online activity through Facebook, a company driven by advertising. Moreover, each service provider wanted to build and maintain relationships directly with their clients, without relying on a third party.

There's general agreement that each user should be able to manage their own online identity securely, across multiple locations, in a way that allows personal information to remain under their control. This is known as "self-sovereign identity."

Self-sovereign identity remains the holy grail of digital identity. In its ideal state, it would allow each of us to have complete control over our online identity, determining what information can be shared and what information remains private, and allowing data to flow across multiple accounts with our consent with minimal human intervention. Not surprisingly, there's still no consensus over how this can be achieved.

One of the early thought leaders in digital identity was the late Canadian computer scientist Kim Cameron, who once held the title Architect of Identity at Microsoft. In 2004, he wrote a landmark piece called "The Laws of Identity" in which he listed seven principles for user-centric digital identity:

1. User control and consent – technical identity systems must only reveal information identifying a user with the user's consent.

2. Minimal disclosure for a constrained use – the solution that discloses the least amount of identifying information and best limits its use is the most stable long-term solution.

3. Justifiable parties – digital identity systems must be designed so the disclosure of identifying information is limited to parties having a necessary and justifiable place in the given identity relationship.

4. Directed identity – a universal identity system must support both "omni-directional" identifiers for use by public entities and "unidirectional" identifiers for use by private entities, thus facilitating discovery while preventing unnecessary release of correlation handles.

5. Pluralism of operators and technologies – a universal identity system must channel and enable the inter-working of multiple identity technologies run by multiple identity providers.

6. Human integration – the universal identity metasystem must define the human user to be a component of the distributed system integrated through unambiguous human–machine communication mechanisms offering protection against identity attacks.

7. Consistent experience across contexts – the unifying identity metasystem must guarantee its users a simple, consistent experience while enabling separation of contexts through multiple operators and technologies.[15]

Cameron developed these principles early in the 2000s, and some twenty years later, there's still no alignment on how to do this. Many people who have tried to tackle the problem have been frustrated by the many competing interests. Personal information has come to be a major source of wealth creation in the digital economy that enterprises (businesses, companies, institutions or organizations) are trying to gain access to however they can. Commercial centralized identity authorities are not trusted to have control over people's personal information and keep it safe. Government authorities are not trusted to keep it private. And people have been unwilling to make the effort to manage their digital identities themselves. Today, the question of who should bear the cost of developing and maintaining a digital identity system remains unanswered, while the number of competitors trying to claim the space continues to grow, adding to the difficulty of finding a universal solution.

Information technology professionals have a saying: "projects can be delivered with quality, speed or economy." You can have any two of the three, but one of them (quality, delivery or cost) will be compromised. It's the same with digital identity, except the trade-offs are security, convenience and cost. The password solution can deliver convenient, low-cost authentication – but without much security. Using complex passwords can provide security at a low cost – but sacrifices convenience. Third-party verification, such as that provided by password managers, can combine security with convenience – but only at a price. So far, users have been unwilling to compromise on cost or convenience, which leaves a secure authentication solution out of reach.

### Fighting Digital Fraud – Account Opening

Financial institutions are acutely aware of their fraud challenges. In the past, new accounts required a personal visit to a physical branch where identity could be verified with physical credentials – "what you are" and "what you have." In the digital world, the identity battle is waged on two fronts. One challenge is establishing whether someone opening a new account is indeed who they claim to be, or if they are using fictitious or stolen information. The second challenge is determining whether a customer logging in to an existing account is in fact the authorized account owner, or someone who has stolen their credentials.

Like any commercial enterprise, a financial institution welcoming you as a client needs your information in order to manage communication and interaction, and must also protect your account from unauthorized access. Unlike other enterprises, it has a legal obligation to establish your identity to reduce the risk of financial crime, money laundering and terrorist financing. In most jurisdictions, regulations specify requirements for identity verification when an account is opened at a financial institution. In Canada, the federal government's Financial Transactions and Reports Analysis Centre (FINTRAC) lists five acceptable methods to verify a client's identity:

1. Examining an authentic, valid, current government-issued photo identification document in the presence of the person being identified. The document must indicate their name, include a photo of them, have a unique identifying number, and match the name and appearance of the person being identified.

2. Matching the name, address and date of birth of the person against a valid, current credit file from a Canadian credit bureau. The file must have been in existence for at least three years and contain information derived from more than one source.

3. Using information from two of the following:

   a. A reliable source that includes the person's name and address, and matches the name and address provided

   b. A reliable source that includes the person's name and date of birth, and matches the name and date of birth provided

   c. A source that includes the person's name and account with a regulated financial institution, and matches the name and account information provided

4. Matching the name, address and date of birth against information in the records of an affiliate that has previously verified the person's identity using an approved method.

5. Relying on identity verification carried out by an entity with which there is an agreement for verifying a person's identity.[16]

For a fraudster to meet FINTRAC requirements when opening a bank account in person, they must have stolen or forged credentials that match their appearance and be in possession of the victim's personal information. More importantly, the fraudster must be capable of impersonating the victim. In person, both "what you are" and "what you have" serve to verify identity, setting a relatively high bar for a fraudster to clear. This limits the number of attempts a fraudster can make, as the process is time-consuming.

In the digital realm, where no real-world interaction occurs, the fraudster need only present "what you know" in the form of information about the individual named on the account. With automation, many attempts to open accounts are possible from anywhere in the world. Since it costs a bank between $250 and $350 to open an account in branch,[17] there is a strong incentive for banks to support digital account opening – an opportunity that fraudsters exploit.

What can a financial institution do to verify identity during an online application for a new account or new service? In keeping with FINTRAC guidelines, the primary approach to verification is matching the name, address and date of birth information presented against information from independent third-party databases, such as credit bureaus, utilities or other financial institutions. This type of verification can rule out synthetic identities – ones that don't exist – but it will fail to expose someone using stolen identity information, so long as the name, address and date of birth are correct. Thwarting a motivated fraudster who's using stolen information is challenging. While there are ways to enhance security, none of them are foolproof:

## 1. Credit bureau identity verification services

Credit bureaus offer a service that verifies identity by asking questions related to the individual's credit history. In addition to matching name, address and date of birth to information in an individual's credit file, the bureau will challenge the applicant with questions such as "Which institution was your mortgage with five years ago?" or "Did you have a car loan in 2015?" This raises the bar for fraudsters, but trial and error, research and phishing are all tools fraudsters will use to pass these tests.

## 2. Document scanning

An applicant can be taken through a process requiring them to scan a piece of government-issued identification, such as a driver's licence, and submit it for verification. This can be enhanced by requiring a selfie to be taken using a smartphone camera, which is then matched against the photo on the driver's licence. Techniques such as "liveness detection" enhance the reliability of the selfie.

While this would appear to add "what you are" and "what you have" to what's already been presented in an application, the relying party only receives digital images, which could, in theory, have been stored, doctored or entirely computer-generated. There's also the challenge of distinguishing between a "real" driver's licence and one that's been altered or forged. While there is software that aims to differentiate forged documents from real ones, fraudsters are busy developing their own software to create increasingly convincing fakes.

## 3. Address verification

For applications requiring high levels of security, the relying party may choose to mail a verification code to the individual at the street address used in the application. This can help ensure that the person is indeed at the address provided, although fraudsters have been known to intercept or redirect mail to steal verification codes. This is also considered a "high friction" approach that could frustrate many applicants.

A lighter version of this approach uses a code sent to the applicant's mobile phone to ensure that the applicant is in possession of the device linked to the number provided in the application. This approach can be enhanced by confirming that the phone number is registered to the individual and the code has not been redirected – but more about that later!

## Fighting Digital Fraud – Account Access

Once an account has been linked to a verified identity, the challenge becomes ensuring that account access is restricted to the authorized owner. At a minimum, this takes a username and password, although, as we now know, this is far from secure. People are notorious for selecting simple passwords and often reusing them, making it easier for fraudsters to guess. Even users of secure passwords are vulnerable to social engineering attacks aimed at exposing their passwords to fraudsters, such as the phishing scams that send out emails informing people of a PayPal refund or suspicious credit card transaction, with a link asking them to log in to their account. The link takes the individual to the fraudster's website where the fraudster captures the login credentials. Such scams have grown increasingly creative and persist because they are effective.

In addition to phishing, malware can be installed on devices to capture keystrokes as passwords are entered. Public Wi-Fi services can be spoofed, tricking people into using a fraudster's site when they think they are logging in to their financial institution. Finally, databases of passwords can be hacked, with passwords then released for sale on the dark web.

So, what can a bank do to protect itself and its clients from accounts being accessed with stolen login credentials? Banks try to recognize their clients by installing software in the form of "tokens" on their devices, banks can also scan the devices to build a profile of applications and browsing history to "fingerprint" them, allowing for returning devices to be identified. Neither approach is foolproof. Software updates can wipe out tokens and alter device fingerprints; hardware upgrades, also common, will have the same effect. People also access accounts from unfamiliar devices. Moreover, anything visible to the bank over an internet connection is also visible to a malicious actor; if they can see it, they can duplicate it to impersonate the victim's device. It's especially difficult to re-authenticate a client with a new device – and fraudsters typically exploit the weakest point in an institution's defences.

One approach has been adding "what you have" to "what you know" in the form of second factor authentication, also known as two-factor authentication or 2FA. Adding a physical item, like a key to unlock a door, is a powerful addition to the authentication process. Email addresses are not linked to physical devices, but phone numbers are, so proving you are in possession of a phone with a specified number helps verify identity. Since most people have their mobile phones with them at all times, this is most commonly done by sending an OTP over the mobile short message service (SMS) – text messaging – confirming that the person logging in is in possession of the client's mobile phone. A fraudster with hacked or stolen login credentials will no longer be able to access the account unless they also steal the victim's phone, which significantly raises the bar for anyone seeking unauthorized account access.

The mobile phone is particularly well suited to two-factor authentication by SMS OTP, since an active phone is unique and hard to duplicate. Each mobile device has a mobile phone number and a subscriber identity module (SIM) card. The mobile phone number is a unique identifier that will connect to only one device.

Two-factor authentication by SMS OTP is used to verify sensitive, high-value or suspicious transactions, or it can be used to verify every login with a username and password. This gives digital account access security equivalent to using a bank card and PIN to verify a transaction. Two-factor authentication by SMS OTP has become so pervasive that, in 2020, it was reported that over half of global text traffic consisted of verification codes.

Fraudsters, being creative and resourceful, have devised ways to overcome two-factor authentication by taking control of the mobile accounts of their intended victims. In addition to stealing the phone, there are two ways to do this. The most common is the SIM swap. The mobile phone number is linked to the phone by the SIM card; the card itself has a unique identifier that the network operator uses to link the phone to the network, and the operator also assigns the client's mobile number to the SIM card. In SIM swap fraud, the fraudster reassigns the client's mobile number to a SIM card under the fraudster's control.

There are a few ways this can be done. A fraudster can contact the mobile network operator and, impersonating the mobile subscriber, claim that they've lost or broken their SIM card and request a new one. Persuasive fraudsters have convinced operators to issue new SIM cards with the victim's mobile number, and once this card is inserted into an active phone, it will override the legitimate owner's control of the mobile number. Since the legitimate owner's phone will still work on Wi-Fi, it may take some time for them to discover that they no longer have a connection to the public network. Meanwhile, all phone and SMS traffic is routed to the fraudster's phone, allowing them to intercept SMS OTP verification codes and enabling them to access bank accounts with stolen credentials, despite two-factor authentication.

Some mobile network operators have implemented self-serve SIM replacement from their websites as a customer service feature; in this case, the fraudster can phish or steal login credentials to a mobile subscriber's account and execute the SIM change online. In addition to a SIM swap, a mobile account can be taken over by a fraudulent number port. Number portability allows subscribers to take their mobile number with them when they switch service providers. Armed with stolen mobile account information, and perhaps a fake ID, a fraudster can request that a number be moved to a new account – in some markets, if it's a prepaid account, little if any personal information is required to open it. Once again, the number will be moved to the fraudster's phone, and the legitimate owner of the number will lose access to the public network. When they realize what's happened, a call into customer service is usually all it takes to have service "snapped back" to the rightful owner, but in the meantime, the fraudster has been using the hijacked service to defeat the two-factor authentication that was protecting financial accounts.

Two-factor authentication can also be delivered by authenticator apps. Some of them can generate verification codes; others prompt the subscriber to use their phone's face or fingerprint authentication capability. These apps, however, may require re-authentication after hardware or software upgrades, and they can be frustrated by malware on some devices.

The key to reliable two-factor authentication is ensuring that the right device receives the authentication request. The mobile network operator and phone's hardware or operating system supplier (for example, Apple, Google or Samsung) are the parties best able to reliably deliver an authentication request to the intended device. While there are ways for fraudsters to try and hijack the verification request, this adds work, making two-factor authentication a valuable, if not foolproof, way to secure logins.

## Fighting Digital Fraud – Privacy

In most cases of identity theft, the fraudster impersonates the victim to make a transaction that benefits the fraudster, leaving the costs and obligations with the victim. This can be as simple as purchasing something with a stolen credit card or more complex, like impersonating a property owner to sell or mortgage a property without the real owner's knowledge. In the real world, this requires significant effort and planning; in the digital world, it requires access to the victim's information.

The US Department of Commerce's National Institute of Standards and Technology defines "personally identifiable information" as information that can be used to distinguish or trace an individual's identity—such as a name, social security number or biometric data records—either alone or in combination with other personal or identifying information that is linked or linkable to a specific individual (date and place of birth, mother's maiden name, etc.).[18] Having someone's PII allows a fraudster to impersonate them to open or access an account, or carry out a transaction. Anecdotal information about family members, travel or hobbies can help fraudsters convince customer service staff that they are who they say they are, helping them change account information, reset passwords or access accounts. This type of information can often also be gleaned from social networks.

Over the last few decades, there's been a dramatic shift in the approach towards personal privacy. Not long ago, names, addresses and phone numbers were regularly published and distributed in telephone directories; now, governments across the globe are implementing legislation to protect personal information. This usually consists of requirements to collect only as much information as is needed, to use it only for the purpose for which it was collected, to keep it only as long as required and to make it only available to those who require it. Information must only be collected with the subject's consent, and they must be made aware of what information is collected and its intended purpose. The party collecting the information must also implement appropriate technical and organizational measures to protect the personal data provided. There is legislation enforcing this in place, to varying degrees, in the United States, the United Kingdom, Canada, the European Union and other jurisdictions.

Why this governmental concern over personal privacy? In the digital age, each of us has interactions with websites and applications hosted by governments, commercial organizations, technology providers, streaming services and social networks. Each relationship comes with its own lengthy set of terms and conditions. When confronted with the terms and conditions, most of us choose convenience over security, skip over the details, agree to the terms and conditions, and adopt the service. Recognizing that this would give licence for widespread capture and distribution of personal information, governments stepped in to develop guidelines for the protection of privacy. The importance of protecting personal information, however, remains poorly understood by the general population.

In 2022, the average American had eighty apps on their smartphone and used ten each day.[19] Apps can collect personal information and even track location, although not all of them do that. In 2022, after a two-year investigation, the Canadian federal privacy commissioner found that a mobile app issued by the restaurant chain Tim Hortons collected customer data without obtaining adequate consent from users.[20] The investigation was launched after the *Financial Post* reported that the app tracked users' locations even when the app was not in use. The restaurant chain stopped collecting location data and tightened contractual protections with their app developers governing personal information.

Joseph Turow, a professor of media systems and industries at the Annenberg School for Communication, studied privacy during digital interactions. He described the challenge in his 2003 report *Americans and Online Privacy: The System is Broken.*

> Companies continually troll for, and exploit, personally identifiable and non-personally identifiable information on the internet. They often begin by getting the names and email addresses of people who sign up for web sites. They can then associate this basic information with a small text file called a cookie that can record the various activities that the registering individual has carried out online during that session and later sessions. Tracking with cookies is just the beginning, however. By using other technologies such as web bugs, spyware, chat-room analysis and transactional database software, web entities can follow people's email and keyboard activities and serve ads to them even when they are off-line. Moreover, companies can extend their knowledge of personally identifiable individuals by purchasing information about them from list firms off the web and linking the information to their own databases. That added knowledge allows them to send targeted editorial matter or advertising to consumers. More specificity also increases the value of the databases when they are marketed to other interested data-trollers.[21]

Turow has also spoken about the dangers of sharing information on social media. Being tagged in a high school graduation photo can give fraudsters information about your age, hometown, high school and graduating year. This information can help answer popular security questions or allow fraudsters to contact your friends in order to draw out even more information.[22]

It's no surprise that the public at large doesn't fully understand how personal information is accessed on the internet or how it's protected – most people are quick to trade off security for convenience. A study undertaken with students at the Massachusetts

Institute of Technology found that small incentives were enough to encourage students to share private information. Researchers concluded that "whenever privacy requires additional effort or comes at the cost of a less smooth user experience, participants are quick to abandon technology that would offer them greater protection."[23]

# 3 Your Credit Card Knows Who You Are

Payment is an interface between dichotomous spaces that define identities: the economy and the individual, the market and the home. Modern payment systems also depend on underlying structures that knit the financial to the personal, producing interoperabilities with other information systems that manage the self: there is a reason that payment card fraud is more commonly referred to as "identity theft." Payment produces transactional identities.

Lana Swartz, "Gendered Transactions:
Identity and Payment at Midcentury"

MASTERCARD DESCRIBES ITSELF AS A technology company that processes payments. In the summer of 2023, I attended a demonstration of some of Mastercard's capabilities at its European headquarters in London, England. A large screen displayed a world map featuring green, yellow and red flashing dots; each dot represented a Mastercard transaction, of which there were a billion each day.

The gentleman giving the demonstration explained that each transaction was evaluated in real-time with a risk assessment sent to the processing bank. Green dots were transactions recommended for approval, while red dots were transactions considered high risk. The bank that issued the customer's payment card was ultimately responsible for approving or declining the transaction, but Mastercard was there to help the bank assess the risk. To Mastercard, a customer was an anonymous card number, but that didn't mean information was lacking. For each transaction, Mastercard could see how it was carried out, whether it was a "card present" transaction in a store, verified by the customer's PIN, or an online transaction, with card details entered into the retailer's website. It could see if the account had previously carried out a transaction with the merchant, or if this was a merchant new to the account. It could see the amount of the transaction and the time of day it took place, and the account's transaction history. During the demonstration, a transaction in Vancouver, Canada, was highlighted. It was a purchase for about $12,000 made online at three o'clock in the morning at a merchant new to the account, and it followed a transaction for about $1,000 that had been carried out with another new merchant three minutes earlier. Both transactions were represented by flashing red dots.

Mastercard supports close to 4,000 card-issuing institutions across more than 120 countries, and processes transactions at over 80 million merchant locations. The number of payment credentials managed has exploded with the introduction of "tokenization" – a unique, random, temporary stand-in number called a token that is stored on the person's device, replacing the credit card's real 16-digit number so it's not shared online. It used to be that each cardholder just had a card with a Mastercard account number; this card could be presented at a merchant location, and the card number could be used to make a remote transaction. While cardholders still have account numbers, they also have additional tokens mapped to their account. These tokens are delivered to their smartphones, watches and laptops, and now tokens are enabling payment from cars, refrigerators and smart appliances too.

Until the middle of the twentieth century, everyday transactions were mainly conducted with cash, with personal cheques used for larger amounts. If the customer had an established relationship with the merchant and demonstrated an ability to pay, the store might run a line of revolving credit or open an account. Legend has it that, in 1949, salesman Frank McNamara found himself entertaining clients in New York City after leaving his wallet at home. To avoid embarrassment, he called his wife, who drove in from Long Island "with cash in her pocket and a hot look in her eye."[24] Soon afterwards, he and his partner Ralph Schneider sought to prevent the recurrence of such embarrassment by launching Diners Club, the first modern charge card, in 1950. Within the first year, there were over 10,000 holders of a cardboard card that could be used in twenty-eight restaurants and two hotels.[25]

American Express entered the 1950s dealing solely in money orders and travellers' cheques, but seeing the success of Diners Club, it launched a charge card in 1958. Later that year, the Bank of America issued a paper BankAmericard granting 60,000 of its clients a preapproved spending limit of $300 with participating merchants. Other banks followed suit, and Americans had the ability to charge expenses, carrying a balance from month to month. Another group of banks formed the Interbank Card Association and introduced a card branded Master Charge in 1969. The banks associated with Bank of America rebranded their card in 1976 as Visa. In 1979, the second group of banks rebranded their card as Mastercard.

What actually is a credit card? It's a credential that identifies an individual as a bank client who can be trusted for future payment. "A 1957 study on payment cards reported that the charge card had become 'a symbol of inexhaustible potency.' It enabled the holder to demonstrate his trustworthiness and membership – to be known – anywhere the card was accepted."[26]

American Express capitalized on this aspect of the payment card in an advertising campaign that ran in the 1970s and 1980s. Using celebrities who were well known by name but not by sight – people like author Stephen King and Garfield cartoonist Jim Davis – the commercials asked, "Do you know me?" Identities remained unclear until their American Express cards were produced, revealing their names.

The payment card enables retail transactions without money changing hands. Multiple parties are involved in a credit card transaction, but four of them do the heavy lifting, giving the business model its name as the "four-party model." The four parties are the cardholder, the cardholder's bank, the merchant and the merchant's bank (or merchant acquirer). When the cardholder presents a card, the merchant, by way of the merchant's bank, sends the cardholder's account information and purchase amount to the cardholder's bank, seeking confirmation that the bank will accept the charge. If the charge is accepted, the merchant receives authorization to complete the transaction, and the cardholder's bank will send payment to the merchant's bank, later settling with the cardholder by way of a monthly bill.

Transactions in a physical location, a store or restaurant, rely on the presentation of a physical card – "what you have" – for identification. In the 1970s, merchants began accepting payment cards for remote transactions; originally they were made over the phone. Remote transactions rely only on account information – "what you know" – and account information is far more easily stolen and replicated than a physical card. Remote or "card not present" transactions have been responsible for a disproportionately large share of credit card fraud since their inception. Banks and card associations have been focused on improving security of both physical cards and card-not-present transactions since cards were introduced.

## Card-Present Transactions

Retailers used to require a signature to secure a credit card transaction, and it was the responsibility of the individual retailer to ensure the card was genuine and the signature provided matched the one on the card. Transactions were sent to the bank for authorization at the end of each day, so if a fraudster was able to convince the retailer to accept a stolen or cloned card, it could take days for the serving bank to authorize or decline it. The 1970s saw the introduction of tamper-resistant signature panels on credit cards, but it was not until the 1980s that real-time authorization was enabled, allowing retailers to decline cards that were reported lost, stolen or over their spending limit.

No matter whether the card was embossed or equipped with a magnetic stripe, the information required to duplicate a card was easily accessible to anyone who got their hands on it, and cloned cards became a major source of payment fraud. In the 1990s, Visa, Mastercard and Europay began work on improving card security with a standardized design for a tamperproof chip, called EMV (for Eurocard, Mastercard and Visa). Specifications for the EMV chip were issued in 1994. The small, square EMV chip on each physical card has a microprocessor, memory and application software, and generates a unique code for each transaction. The chip was designed with security in mind, protecting the transaction codes with powerful cryptography and requiring the cardholder's PIN authorization.

The introduction of chip and PIN cards has virtually eliminated credit card fraud at retail locations where chip and PIN terminals are used. In 2015, the United States began implementing chip and PIN cards in retail, and the US Federal Reserve reported that the fraud rate of card-present payments and withdrawals involving a

PIN was less than one-third the fraud rate of card-present payments without a PIN in the first year of introduction.[27] By 2019, Visa reported an 87 percent decline in card-present fraud, with the remaining fraud concentrated in locations where the chip and PIN were not yet adopted.

Putting a secure credential in the hands of the customer ("what you have"), combined with a unique personal identification number ("what you know"), has proven to be a powerful and effective combination for verifying the identity of cardholders for retail transactions. It has virtually eliminated identity-related fraud when cards are presented for payment.

## Card-Not-Present Transactions

A card-not-present transaction is a transaction that's carried out remotely, without the physical card being presented to the merchant. Such transactions were first conducted over the phone, or by mail, but are now mostly carried out online. The transaction relies on the presentation of cardholder information only – "what you know" – and does not verify "what you have," making it more susceptible to fraud.

Historically, card information was not very closely guarded. For decades, a credit card transaction slip taken from an embossed card contained the cardholder's name, card number and expiry date, everything needed to clone a card. Cards were handed to serving staff in bars and restaurants, to gas station attendants and to staff in other enterprises, who would disappear before returning with a transaction slip to be signed. There was ample opportunity for card information to be captured by anyone inclined to steal it. Banks had to either look for credit card fraud by questioning unusual transactions or rely on cardholders to identify transactions they did not make after a card had been compromised.

Over time, measures were taken to improve the security of card-not-present payments. The card verification value (CVV), a three- or four-digit number, was introduced on the back of the card to add information that was not recorded on a retail credit card slip; the CVV had to be read off the back of the card when making a purchase over the phone. Soon afterwards, the cardholder's billing address was made available to merchants for additional verification. Later, the practice of truncating card numbers (replacing some numbers with placeholders such as asterisks) on receipts was introduced to limit their exposure, while at the same time, banks and card associations started using analytics to help identify suspicious or unusual transactions.

These measures were not enough to eliminate card-not-present fraud, and card associations continued with their efforts. One attempt by Visa was the addition of a layer of username and password verification known as Verified by Visa, which called for the cardholder to establish an account with Visa in addition to the card account they had with their financial institution. For online transactions, the cardholder would see a popup that required them to sign in to their Visa account before the transaction was sent for processing. While this offered an added layer, it was no different than the tools tech-savvy banks already had in place; the fraudsters just had to get their hands on a little more login information. Furthermore, the process created a new database of cardholder personal information and card numbers held by Visa. Collecting and storing this information added to the number of places fraudsters could hack into. The additional password also increased customer confusion and led to frustration when transactions were declined. Verified by Visa was replaced by Visa 3-D Secure, which required no customer registration and instead relied on more data exchange between the merchant and card issuer, such as merchandise details, shipping location and device type, to determine whether the transaction was consistent with the cardholder's profile.

Using analytics and probabilities to evaluate transactions resulted in a mathematical war of attrition in which the card associations and financial institutions had to trade off two types of errors. False positives were unusual-but-legitimate transactions that were declined because they did not appear consistent with the cardholder's profile – they looked like fraud, even though they weren't. Both banks and merchants wanted to minimize false positives since they often led to purchases being abandoned, frustrated customers and lost revenue. Relaxing the algorithms to minimize false positives, however, leaves a window of opportunity that fraudsters can exploit by increasing the number of attacks, which is relatively easy to do with automation.

## Tokenization

New technology has created ways to add security to card-not-present transactions, and tokenization is one of them. As mentioned earlier, it's the process of replacing a cardholder's primary credential (credit card information and cardholder data) with a unique, limited-use string of numbers so the credentials are not exposed during payment. A trusted authority holds the cardholder's account information and has a link to the cardholder's device, usually secured by a unique, cryptographically identified app. The cardholder is able to link multiple devices to their card account, each verified by the authority and identified by a separate and unique token. The merchant is also required to establish a secure link to the trusted authority and create a dedicated checkout option for clients. When the cardholder makes a purchase, they choose the checkout option specific to their authority and identify themselves to the merchant with the token on their device. The merchant passes the token to the trusted authority, which verifies the token and confirms the requested transaction through their link to the cardholder's device. This results in a very secure payment process with many benefits.

You may recognize the process as the one used by PayPal. PayPal acts as the trusted authority; the cardholder registers their payment information with PayPal and maintains a PayPal app on their device, which allows PayPal to verify transactions with the cardholder. Merchants must establish and maintain a PayPal checkout option. Once a client chooses PayPal at the checkout, the merchant sends the client's request to PayPal for verification, and PayPal confirms payment.

In this process, PayPal is the only party that sees and holds the cardholder's name, address and card details. There's much less risk of exposure to hacking if each and every merchant does not hold or manage cardholder information. PayPal also ensures the legitimacy of connected merchants, which eliminates the possibility of a cardholder's details being sent to a fraudulent website that would steal their funds or data. PayPal provides secure shipping information as well, without the merchant having to collect it for each client. Finally, if one of the tokens is stolen or hacked, it's essentially useless to the fraudster: trying to use it without PayPal authentication would result in a declined transaction, and PayPal would not approve a transaction that had not been verified by its client. Even if a PayPal client's device were lost or stolen, only the token on that device would have to be cancelled. They wouldn't have to cancel any payment cards or deal with suppliers relying on recurring card payments.

If this is as good as it sounds, why isn't everyone using it? Securely managing multiple tokens with millions of clients and multiple retailers is a significant data processing task. Only recently has the capability become available to perform it at the scale and transaction times required by payment processors. Moreover, clients need to download an app to their mobile devices, register for the service and establish their identity with the trusted authority. Unless you're willing to go through a strong authentication procedure at registration, the process has no fraud reduction benefit. Merchants also have to establish secure links to the trusted authority and provide a dedicated checkout option. Building such an ecosystem is a significant challenge – only a small number of brands can pull it off.

PayPal came along when people were still leery of giving their payment card details to online merchants. It quickly became apparent that adding the PayPal checkout option helped reduce shopping cart abandonment and increased sales. Once PayPal was established, merchants saw little benefit from adding other checkout options. Visa tried to replicate PayPal's success with Visa Checkout, and Mastercard tried Masterpass, but both faced an uphill battle against PayPal's first mover advantage – the competitive edge from being the first to offer the service. Merchants did not want the clutter of multiple checkout options or the effort of maintaining secure connections with a larger number of parties unless it delivered a significant benefit. The card associations, with the addition of American Express, have since regrouped and are reported to be collectively planning a service similar to PayPal's.

Two parties have seen success with models similar to PayPal's, but neither has had a quick or easy time of it. Apple Pay started with tokens delivered to a secure element on an iPhone that allowed the phone to emulate a payment card for in-store proximity payments at contactless terminals. Since Apple Pay had card details and a tokenization capability, it could also facilitate online payments at merchants that offered Apple Pay as a checkout option. The Google Wallet provides similar capabilities. It took over ten years for mobile wallets to establish themselves for in-store and online payments, even with the brand strength and marketing reach of Apple and Google. Lesser brands are faced with the challenge of attracting merchants before they have retail clients and of enticing retail clients before they have merchants. There's also the matter of extracting a processing fee to help pay for the service. All in all, building this type of ecosystem is a daunting task that requires significant investment and deep pockets before any hope of breaking even, let alone realizing a return.

We will later look at whether Apple and Google can do for digital identity what they've done for payments, and whether tokenization, with the use of a trusted authority, can be the key to enabling secure digital identity. In the meantime, payment credentials have now been evolving for over seventy years – each added security measure has reduced a type of fraud, but with each reduction, fraudsters have found new opportunities to exploit. Of the many lessons to be learned from payments, the most significant may be that secure verification remains a journey, not a destination.

# 4 Your Phone as Your Avatar

Smartphones are not just gadgets. They have become an
extension of our being, a key to the world we live in.

Jerry Yang, co-founder of Yahoo!

NO OTHER PRODUCT HAS EVOLVED as rapidly as the cell phone:
the journey from two-way radio to personal multimedia terminal took just twenty-five years. In that time, the cell phone
morphed from a simple radio allowing talk across open channels,
easily intercepted by anyone with a scanner, to delivering secure,
encrypted digital transmissions that can unlock doors, make payments, purchase groceries, aid navigation, play music, measure
your heart rate and show movies – and these are only a few of the
continuously expanding range of functions. Does this mean it can
also verify identity in the digital world?

The mobile industry's transformation was not only rapid – it
was also largely unplanned. Initially conceived as a mobile version
of the wired telephone, the first cell phones were large, cumbersome and plagued by limitations. Overcoming these limitations
led to unintended consequences, giving the cell phone capabilities
that made its wired cousin look quaint and antiquated.

The mobile phone started life as an advanced two-way radio. What distinguished it from other radios was its ability to change channels in the middle of a conversation without the speakers noticing, a feature that transformed the mobile phone into a revolutionary device. There were earlier versions of two-way radio telephones, but they were unwieldly car-mounted devices that relied on a mobile operator to place calls. More importantly, they used scarce radio channels over wide areas, drastically limiting the number of calls that could be carried at any one time. This limited number of calls (or units of service) denied the industry the scale needed to drive down costs and improve performance. Then came a breakthrough: confining each unit's use of a radio channel to a much smaller individual cell allowed the same radio channel to be reused for other calls in other cells. This distribution of channels across cells gave the technology its name: "cellular." The ability to reuse spectrum (a range of frequencies) dramatically expanded the network's capacity to carry calls, turning a niche business service into a mass market communications phenomenon.

But early cell phone service was not secure from eavesdropping, nor was it an efficient user of radio spectrum, consuming as it did an entire radio channel for each call. Anyone with a radio scanner could browse the airwaves and listen to conversations conducted on mobile phones, much like they could turn a radio dial to tune in to a station.

In the 1990s, stories of intercepted celebrity cell phone conversations were commonplace. In 1992, a UK resident trying out an electronic scanner chanced upon, and recorded, an intimate conversation between Prince Charles and Camilla Parker Bowles, who were both married at the time to other people. The following year, the British press published the entire conversation, giving rise to Camillagate. In 1997, a cellular conversation in which US House Leader Newt Gingrich admitted ethical errors to Republican allies was intercepted by a Florida couple with a scanner, who also recorded the conversation. This, too, made its way to the press and out to the public.

In addition to listening in on conversations, intercepting a call allowed the caller's account information to be discovered, enabling criminals to clone phones, use the services and have the bill sent to unsuspecting subscribers. Cloned phones were also used to buy pay-per-use calling services, which were charged to victims' accounts, with the criminals who owned the calling services pocketing the profits.

Despite the problems with privacy and security, demand for mobile services skyrocketed, and the industry struggled to provide enough bandwidth. Wired phone users were used to getting an intermittent tone (busy signal) if the party they were calling was already on a call. Wireless users soon got used to a quicker intermittent tone (fast busy signal, also called a reorder tone) that occurred when a call could not be placed because a radio channel was not available to connect to the network. The only thing to do was hit the redial button and hope for a channel to open up. Frustration levels were so high that cell phone owners were known to throw their phones from moving vehicles.

To improve the call carrying capacity, voice conversations were digitized. This compressed conversations for transmission so multiple calls could be carried on a single radio channel. While early digital compression reduced the voice quality, it did protect conversations from being intercepted – eavesdropping was no longer possible unless you had the digital compression algorithms. As digitization technologies grew more sophisticated, voice quality improved, but the handsets now required ever more computing power. By the end of the 1990s, a digital mobile phone had the computing power of a laptop computer of the same era. Creative minds went to work thinking of all the ways to put that power to use, including playing music, sending digital messages, taking pictures, storing maps, and other applications. In 2005, The

Economist's *Technology Quarterly* highlighted the mobile phone's increasing sophistication in an article titled "The Device That Ate Everything?"[28]

At the heart of each mobile phone is a subscriber identity module card. Each SIM card has an integrated circuit chip that stores the subscriber information used by the mobile network operator to manage that user's network access and account. The information on the chip is encrypted, with much of its contents accessible only by the network operator; parties connecting over the public airwaves cannot read or access content on the chip, which makes it resistant to hacking and eliminates the cloning of mobile phones. By 2020, the global mobile industry was serving billions of unique subscribers, allowing each to reliably send and receive messages, no matter where they were in the world. SIM cards reliably identified each subscriber and securely enabled networks to direct and manage their traffic.

The SIM card not only affords the mobile phone a unique and secure credential, but in most cases, it's also associated with the handset owner's personal identity. Most common in the United States, Canada and many European countries are "postpaid" accounts – holders of the accounts must sign contracts with their service providers, which verify their identity and bill the accounts for their use, typically monthly. Most of the rest of the world's mobile plans do not have service contracts and are, rather, "prepaid" – these accounts are paid in advance and mobile operators maintain them so long as they're funded, requiring neither contract nor an account holder's identity. However, by 2021, driven by security concerns, 157 countries introduced mandatory policies that required customers on all mobile phone plans, prepaid included, to register their SIMs with verified identities.[29] According to the GSMA (which supports and promotes the global system for mobile communications), 82 percent of the world's SIM cards are registered with a confirmed identity, making the SIM the single most common identity credential in the world.[30]

In addition to confirming identity, the SIM card is actively managed. The network operator associates it with a mobile phone and monitors the phone's location, network status and usage, and whether the account is in good standing for payment. If the phone is lost or stolen, the owner can alert the service provider, and the account will be suspended or cancelled. Since the mobile phone is typically a personal rather than shared device, the owner of the phone usually has it with them, or at least within arm's reach, making awareness of any issues with the device usually immediate.

The mobile phone has had a profound effect on lifestyle. In 1995, when the majority of the world's phones were fixed land-lines, less than half the world's population had ever made a single phone call. Just twenty years later, over half the people on the planet owned a phone of their own. No longer were we calling a house or office and asking to speak to a person, we were calling the person. We could also send a message to the person directly, rather than having a message left at a place.

The mobile phone is now far from just a phone: it's an internet-connected communicator with an assigned phone number. The mobile number not only directs calls and messages, it acts as an identity credential.

"What you have" provides stronger verification than "what you know" because physical things are harder to steal than information and can't easily be copied. When any account is linked to a mobile phone number, demonstrating possession of the phone can help verify account ownership. The most common example of this is a text message or one-time pass code sent to a phone to prove possession of the device.

In most cases, the mobile network operator also has their sub-scriber's name and address. With the customer's consent, the operator can provide this information to verify identity and even fill out forms if the account owner is applying for a new service. This saves time, avoids keystroke errors and assures the new service provider that information has been supplied by a reliable source.

Moreover, a mobile subscriber applying for any online service can have their identity confirmed by the mobile network operator. The new supplier can submit the mobile number with the applicant's name and address to the mobile network operator, who then compares that with the information on file for that mobile account. While customer consent is required to allow the mobile network operator to provide verification as a service, it helps protect the subscriber by ensuring that their personal information is not being used by a fraudster.

Another powerful application is the use of the mobile number to authorize a mobile-initiated login attempt. When someone logs in to a service from a mobile device, the service provider just sees an anonymous IP address, rather than the mobile phone number. However, on request, and with customer consent, the mobile network operator can disclose the number of the device being used. Since this verification comes directly from the network, it means the number can't be spoofed or tampered with in any way, and can form the foundation for "passwordless" account access, user-friendly two-factor authentication or simply enhanced security for all transactions.

With such strong potential, you might wonder why the mobile phone doesn't already play an even greater role in identity verification. Well, it turns out that mobile network operators have not made using phones for that purpose very easy.

### Industry Fragmentation

In 2022, the mobile industry association, the GSMA, listed 782 mobile network operator members across 220 countries. In most countries, there were three or four major operators, and in many markets, the operators had sub-brands running as independent suppliers. Moreover, many operators supported mobile virtual network operators – independent resellers that market wireless services to their own customers. An enterprise wanting to use mobile network information for identity verification might have to connect to four or five separate mobile networks in each market to cover its customer base, but there's little chance that networks will present their customer information in similar formats or provide device information in consistent ways. Each network will have its own requirements for a secure connection, its own requirements for collecting customer consent and its own standards for treatment of personal information. Different pricing structures and service levels across networks further complicate business arrangements. For a company operating in a single market, this is challenging; for an international brand, it's enough to make them look for other solutions.

The mobile industry recognized these challenges and took steps to address them. Mobile Connect was launched in 2014 to help digital service providers authenticate users and confirm identity. Deployed by over seventy mobile networks since its launch, Mobile Connect is a portfolio of standardized secure identity services for authenticating users, authorizing transactions, verifying identity, and confirming user and device attributes. The standards simplify the task of dealing with multiple mobile operators, but separate connections and business relationships with each operator are still required.

In Canada, the national mobile network operators went even further by creating EnStream, a joint venture that provides access to 90 percent of the country's mobile users for identity verification through a single point of contact. This has helped Canadian banks and service companies adopt mobile identity and device verification faster than enterprises operating in international markets.

The complexities of connecting to multiple mobile operators across different geographic regions created an opportunity for tech companies to step in as resellers of mobile network operator verification services. These include providers of SMS services, new suppliers of identity services and global aggregators of carrier information, which provide seamless connectivity to multiple mobile operators. But even these companies are finding that dealing with multiple mobile operators is challenging.

In 2023, companies such as Prove, Telesign, Sinch, Sekura.id were among those racing to build large footprints of coverage to position themselves as preferred suppliers of mobile verification to international companies. Some aggregators were offering access to operators that served over two billion mobile subscribers in total but weren't always able to combine a large client base with a high percentage of users covered in individual markets. The race is still on to offer coverage that is universally broad and deep; until such access is available, establishing carrier verification services in international markets will remain a complex undertaking.

## Market Coverage

While there are 157 countries in which every mobile SIM card is registered to a proven identity, this is not the case in the United States, the United Kingdom, Canada and sixty other countries, where only the identities of contracted subscribers are verified. Many accounts are managed at a household or small business level, with only the primary account holder verified. Close to half of the subscriber base in some areas may be on shared, company or prepaid plans, making it hard to rely solely on mobile information for identity verification. When the carrier has a proven identity, verification can be fast and reliable. But when the mobile account is part of a group plan, the relying party must resort to other means – another reason some organizations have not embraced mobile verification. While it's true that mobile data doesn't entirely cover any market, so far there is no data source with that kind of complete coverage.

The mobile industry is addressing the coverage concern by making its verification services available to identity companies that combine mobile with other identity sources. Having access to multiple data sources makes it easier for suppliers to offer a full-service solution, although larger, more resourceful enterprises often choose to have relationships with multiple data suppliers and build complete coverage solutions themselves.

## Privacy and Security

In the digital age, most jurisdictions have stepped up legislation governing privacy and the use of personal information. The European Union has put in place the General Data Protection Regulation (GDPR) to govern the access to and use of personal information for anyone doing business in or with European countries. Similar laws are in place in most other countries. GDPR requires that people be informed of how their data will be used and must opt in to allow its use. Personal data can only be used for the permitted purpose and must not be retained once that purpose has been fulfilled.

Mobile operators hold customer information so they can deliver their service to their subscribers and manage the commercial relationship. Any data use beyond this requires the customer's permission, so a company trying to verify personal information associated with a mobile account must first get the mobile subscriber's consent, then submit proof of this to the mobile operator along with the verification request. In practice, most mobile operators hold suppliers of verification services to even higher standards than those required by law to avoid public concern over improper use of personal information. The reputational damage would be greater than any value the mobile operator could gain from the verification services.

In addition to addressing privacy concerns, mobile operators must keep the connections to their systems secure. This includes vetting the connected parties to make sure they operate secure facilities and using network connections that encrypt traffic to protect it from interception.

## EnStream – A Case Study

The modest office building at 55 University Avenue in Toronto's downtown core is considered a class-B building in commercial real estate circles. There, on the second floor, is a small, but unusual, tech company familiar to few Canadians, although many benefit from its services. What makes EnStream unusual is that it's a joint venture of Canada's three national wireless companies – Bell, Rogers and TELUS. While the global telecom industry has tried joint ventures before, they have not lasted or seen success. Almost twenty years since it was established, EnStream continues to defy the odds.

Canada is a vast, sparsely populated nation. Canadian wireless operators have had to find creative ways to deal with opportunities beyond the scope of any individual carrier. When text messaging was first introduced, it was only possible to send messages to subscribers on the same network. The Canadian industry was early to boost usage by introducing intercarrier messaging, which allowed subscribers to send and receive messages between different mobile networks. To reduce the cost of expanding coverage, Canadian networks were also early to share infrastructure between competitors. When using a mobile phone to make payments was first proposed, it was recognized that the service could not be done by one carrier acting alone. No retailer would use the capability if it only worked with the phones of one mobile operator. Seeing potential for mobile payments, the carriers joined forces to develop a payment service.

In 2004, years before the iPhone, let alone Apple Pay, it was not clear how a phone could make payments. At the time, as vice-president of business development for one of the networks, I was tasked with working with my counterparts at the other carriers to figure this out and develop a business plan. We came to realize that we couldn't get retailers interested in the idea, so we settled on finding a way to fund prepaid phone accounts directly from a mobile phone. In 2005, Bell, Rogers and TELUS created Wireless Payment Services (WPS) to do just that, and I joined my counterparts from the other carriers on the board of directors.

From its inception, WPS faced challenges. The original vision of topping up a prepaid account by transferring funds directly from a bank account was never realized because banks wouldn't allow any site but a banking website to access bank account information. We asked WPS to pivot, rebrand itself as EnStream and create its own mobile payment service, called Zoompass, which used a mobile app for online payments and person-to-person money transfers. Zoompass provided users with a contactless Mastercard for in-store purchases from the same prepaid cash account. At the time, mobile phones were not yet capable of contactless payments, although the mobile industry's "pay by mobile" technology was in development and the future "tap to pay" capability of the phone was on the horizon. We thought Zoompass could be the foundation for the Canadian mobile industry's payment service, once phones were equipped with contactless payment capabilities.

As it happened, Canadian banks were more concerned about competition from Apple and Google than they were about competition from the telcos; the banks were willing to work with us to enable their own plans. At that time, I was asked to take over operations at EnStream. We sold Zoompass to a prepaid card operator and pivoted again to launch a GSMA pay-by-mobile platform to help the banks deliver their own mobile payment services.

The GSMA technology enabled delivery and storage of bank credentials on the secure element found on specialized multi-tenant SIM cards, which can securely host multiple service providers. Payment credentials could be accessed by the phone's near field communication (NFC) antenna – which enabled data exchange between two devices in close proximity of about four centimetres – and allowed bank clients to make contactless payments at retail locations. The pay-by-mobile approach allowed banks to deliver Visa, Mastercard, American Express or Interac credentials directly to a customer's mobile phone so it could be used as a contactless payment card.

EnStream set out to provide payment credential delivery across the entire Canadian wireless industry – a significant undertaking requiring special-purpose platforms that could securely perform complex functions. EnStream's secure element manager (SEM) controlled access to SIM cards and managed encryption keys for five major telcos. A trusted service manager (TSM) encrypted payment card credentials for delivery onto the multi-tenant SIM cards. There were a handful of SIM card manufacturers used by the Canadian mobile industry, each with their own technical idiosyncrasies. Many SIM card manufacturers provided their own SEM and TSM technology optimized for their own cards. Visa, Mastercard and American Express were also building facilities optimized for their own credentials, and each demanded rigorous adherence to their own specifications to allow third-party delivery of their credentials.

In spite of these challenges, we succeeded in building a hub that was approved for service by Visa, Mastercard, American Express and Interac, and connected nine financial institutions across five telcos. EnStream's hub incorporated the TSMs of different suppliers and dealt with two different SEM technologies. It was arguably the most successful example anywhere of a GSMA platform delivering financial credentials to mobile network operators.

Success, however, was short-lived. The credential delivery infrastructure was expensive to maintain. Banks discovered that supporting their own payment "wallets" on different mobile operating systems and working with different mobile phone suppliers used a lot of resources and didn't often lead to a satisfying user experience. Moreover, the expected rush to use mobile phones for payment never materialized. When Apple finally introduced Apple Pay as a mobile wallet available for all bank payment cards, banks re-evaluated their approach and began using Apple Pay, which came with its own credential delivery service. Similarly, Google introduced Android Pay for Android devices, and not to be left out, Samsung introduced Samsung Pay. Banks began migrating from their own payment wallets to these open wallets, disconnecting from EnStream.

As this was happening, concerns over digital identity were building. How could a bank know who had requested a credit card for Apple Pay? Using the Apple ID to verify the identity of the requesting party did not meet bank standards, and Apple did not permit banks to access the Apple Wallet directly. After some negotiation, Apple eventually agreed to allow banking apps to verify the identity of anyone requesting a credit card. This was even more problematic on Android devices, where no database existed to verify identity. As a result, in Canada, Bell, Rogers and TELUS began to get requests for identity verification services. The carriers, concerned with issues of customer privacy and aware that this was unlikely to represent a significant business opportunity, passed the opportunity on to EnStream. Fortunately, in EnStream, we already had most of the infrastructure needed to verify mobile account subscriber identities and devices from our legacy pay-by-mobile service. EnStream pivoted once again to focus on verifying mobile devices and identities.

Since 2016, EnStream has, with customer consent, helped verify identities for new digital accounts and ensure the security of mobile devices delivering two-factor authentication. An enterprise accepting an account application online can submit the requesting name, address and mobile number to EnStream, which can verify this data against the information held on file for the associated mobile account. A successful match eliminates synthetic accounts; it does not, however, prevent an applicant from using stolen information. To stop identity thieves, the service provider can send the applicant a one-time passcode by text to make sure they're in possession of the device linked to the number provided. In addition, EnStream can check for signs of mobile account takeover, such as a SIM swap or number port transfer, in case a fraudster has hijacked the account to use the stolen information.

EnStream is arguably the best example of a mobile industry initiative to make network information easy to use for identity verification. Verification services nationwide are available through a single point of contact, covering 90 percent of the mobile devices in the country. Even so, getting people to adopt the service has not been fast or easy. Large client organizations have complex IT systems, and the design and implementation of verification services is equally difficult. Moreover, the large number of verification alternatives available, with yet more in development, makes it hard for enterprises to choose solutions, regardless of how effective they may appear.

What can we learn from the EnStream experience? It's clear that the mobile phone is a proven and effective means of confirming identity. Using the phone for two-factor authentication by SMS OTP is both easy and efficient, but it's also vulnerable to mobile account takeover attacks. Checking with the carrier strengthens this form of two-factor authentication by exposing mobile account takeover, eliminating this vulnerability. Mobile network operators have stringent privacy and security requirements, which makes it challenging to access information for identity verification. The network operators themselves have not had much success managing verification services or launching new ventures with long paybacks. Other carrier joint ventures have been launched but failed to survive; EnStream is unique as the longest running telco joint venture in existence, and the only example of a carrier-owned identity verification service of its kind. Finally, an entire ecosystem of mobile network service aggregators and identity service providers is required to harness the power of the mobile phone for identity verification. Fortunately, this has been recognized by both entrepreneurs and investors, and such an ecosystem is in active development. In time, the mobile device will undoubtedly emerge as a powerful tool for identity verification across the globe.

# 5 Is Social Media Killing Privacy?

It's amazing how much information we share in social media, then we wonder why people steal our identity.

Frank Abagnale, security consultant,
author and convicted felon

FEW THINGS HAVE BEEN EMBRACED as quickly and wholeheartedly by people across the globe as social media networks in the early 2000s. Specialized services for information, news, entertainment and connection to friends and family were all marginalized by this new phenomenon, which began tracking careers, interests, hobbies, tastes and community contacts. Between 2005 and 2018, the percentage of Americans using social networks increased from 5 to 69 percent.[31] At the same time, over 90 percent of Americans felt that they had lost control over how companies were using their personal information, with over 80 percent feeling insecure when sharing information over social media.[32]

Social media networks were accumulating so much information about us that they could discern patterns of behaviour we didn't yet recognize ourselves. Was this a threat to our privacy, a gift to identity thieves or a potential asset for identity verification? Could "sign in with Facebook" provide reliable verification? Before we delve into this, let's take a detour and explore what we mean by privacy.

## Privacy

In theory, privacy (as in "freedom from being observed or disturbed") is a simple concept. In practice, privacy, like liberty or loyalty, can be hard to define with any precision. In his book *Understanding Privacy*, Daniel Solove, the Eugene L. and Barbara A. Bernard Professor of Intellectual Property and Technology Law at the George Washington University Law School, wrote:

> Privacy is a concept in disarray. Nobody can articulate
> what it means. Currently, privacy is a sweeping concept,
> encompassing (among other things) freedom of thought,
> control over one's body, solitude in one's home, control over
> personal information, freedom from surveillance, protec-
> tion of one's reputation, and protection from searches and
> interrogations. Philosophers, legal theorists, and jurists
> have frequently lamented the great difficulty in reaching a
> satisfying conception of privacy. Legal scholar Arthur Miller
> has declared that privacy is "difficult to define because it is
> exasperatingly vague and evanescent." "On closer examina-
> tion," author Jonathan Franzen observes, "privacy proves
> to be the Cheshire cat of values: not much substance, but a
> very winning smile." According to philosopher Julie Inness,
> the legal and philosophical discourse of privacy is in a state
> of "chaos." Professor Hyman Gross asserts that "the concept
> of privacy is infected with pernicious ambiguities." Political
> scientist Colin Bennett declares that "attempts to define
> the concept of 'privacy' have generally not met with any
> success." According to legal theorist Robert Post, "Privacy

is a value so complex, so entangled in competing and contradictory dimensions, so engorged with various and distinct meanings, that I sometimes despair whether it can be usefully addressed at all."[33]

There was little discussion of privacy for most of human history. University of Alabama professor and information privacy professional Lawrence Cappello writes that things changed in the late nineteenth century with the introduction of the Kodak camera and newspapers' newfound ability to print photographs.

For the first time people could walk around taking photographs without having to fumble with large contraptions that needed to be held steady for minutes at a time in front of a willing and frozen participant. Which means that for the first time individuals could suddenly have their likeness captured in public by strangers in a candid and vulnerable fashion without their consent. Then, on the heels of this wondrous technological development came Stephen Henry Horgan's "halftone" process that made possible the widespread reproduction of photographs in newspapers.[34]

The publication of photographs gave rise to the first documented concerns over privacy and led to the first law review of the right to privacy, written by Justice Louis Brandeis in 1890. In this review, privacy was treated as a right to be left alone, as opposed to having one's personal affairs widely publicized in the media. At that time, the debate was over whether photographs of individuals could be taken and published without their consent, and whether personal stories could be printed in papers despite objections. The right to privacy was weighed against the public's right to be informed, and it was the newspapers that ultimately prevailed, with the right to print photographs and stories originating in the public domain without restriction.

The focus on privacy then shifted to the preservation of personal information and personal space, protection from searches and the establishment of laws against disclosure of information. The United Nations Universal Declaration of Human Rights of 1948 stated, "No one shall be subjected to arbitrary interference with his privacy, family, home or correspondence, nor attacks upon his honor and reputation."[35] Many nations, as well as the Organization for Economic Cooperation and Development, the European Union and the Asia-Pacific Economic Cooperation Framework, implemented guidelines and laws to protect privacy.

In the digital age, social media and demands for access to information have fragmented the dialogue on privacy. Some believe that privacy is dead. Others view it as an antisocial construct that only protects the privileged few. Still more dismiss the question, pointing out that privacy may be of interest in the abstract, but it seems to be of little concern to the public, who freely share personal information.

While privacy continues to be debated in legal, social and commercial circles, let's return to the question of social media's impact on privacy and identity.

When I was in business school, back in the 1980s, an executive from a major broadcasting company came to speak to our marketing class about his business. He asked the class to consider what a radio station markets. The class listed music, news, commentary and other forms of content. He dismissed our suggestions. "You," he said, "are what we market. Our customers are advertisers, and they pay us to reach an audience. We attract you with music, news and other forms of content, but that's not what we sell." At that time, agencies conducted surveys to measure how many listeners tuned in to each radio station, together with their demographics. Based on this information, media buyers would purchase advertising space on programming that appealed to their target market.

Social media networks and online search operate on the same business model.

Facebook, Google, X (formerly known as Twitter) and others collect information about us – our interests, our browsing histories, our media habits – but they are not in the business of selling this information. Rather, they are in the business of selling advertisers space on their platforms for delivery of targeted messages on our screens. Digital channels accounted for 60 percent of global advertising expenditures in 2022.[36] An individual's personal information, such as name and address, is not needed to deliver the ads and is not of much interest to media buyers, which would rather know an individual's habits and shopping interests. Unlike the media companies of old, social networks don't need to conduct surveys to track their audience; they have troves of detailed information and can segment their subscribers based on activities, viewing habits, friends, browsing histories and other variables. This gives the social networks incredible advertising power. Add the ability of mobile apps to determine a user's location, and social networks can deliver targeted ads specific to a user's interests as they are out shopping and seeking information.

Since personal information, like name and address, isn't needed to find a specific demographic, social networks have little incentive, or need, to confirm the identity of their users. Advertisers, of course, do care about people seeing their ads, so the networks are motivated to ensure accounts are held by real people – and not bots, the deceased or businesses. Meta reported that approximately 3.2 billion fake accounts were removed from Facebook in 2019.[37] While Facebook and other social networks may not care whether accounts are opened with real identities, they have tried to capitalize on identity verification. "We know you," they proclaim, "so log in with us," encouraging users to use their Facebook credentials and letting Facebook enable registration for new services. This simplifies account management for the user, but it doesn't offer the new relying party any real assurance that the identity provided can be trusted. Opening an account through a social network also benefits that network by providing more information about its client – adding active subscriptions and accounts to their profile. Since logging in with Facebook adds to Facebook's information about users, it comes free of charge. It doesn't, however, provide sites using a Facebook login with any guarantee that people are who they say they are.

It's not hard to establish a fake social media account, and people have many reasons for doing it. They may want support for a synthetic identity, a way of anonymously gathering information on others or a vehicle for posting messages while keeping their identity hidden. Social media sites are increasingly used by employers, colleagues and social contacts to gain insight into a person's character: 78 percent of consumers using dating apps specifically check the profiles of potential dates on social media.[38] A fraudster looking to create a synthetic identity can easily support it with a fake social media account.

Seeing banner advertising for Paris hotels on your phone after you've done a search for airfares may be unsettling, but does targeted advertising based on your digital footprint constitute a privacy concern? If everything is running as intended, it shouldn't – in fact, most people prefer relevant advertising to ads they have no interest in. Social networks don't sell your information to other parties; on the contrary, that information is the foundation of their advertising business, and they protect it. While networks deliver ads, the subscribers themselves can remain anonymous to the world at large. This, however, does not mean that social networks pose no threat to privacy. They can provide fraudsters with information that helps them impersonate their victims; they've been known to be hacked or breached, exposing account information; and they display information that can cause reputational damage.

People use social media to put personal information on public display, and this can lead to unintended consequences. Posting family vacation photographs can let burglars know a house is vacant or inform the press that a public official is not on the job. Fraudsters can use social media to gather answers to knowledge-based questions that relying parties use to verify identity, such as where you went to high school or the town in which you were born. This type of information can help fraudsters successfully impersonate individuals when trying to access bank or telecom accounts.

Social media sites also store personal information, account details and links to other sites, which identity-stealing hackers have found ways to access. In 2022, Ireland's Data Protection Commission slapped Meta with a US$276 million fine for an April 2021 leak that exposed names, birthdates, phone numbers and locations of more than 533 million users.[39]

The belief that people should be able to protect themselves from public scrutiny, held to this day, was the original case for privacy. While content on social networks is self-selected and curated, social norms change over time and vary from place to place. Statements and images, taken out of context, can be damaging to anyone's reputation, and there are few people, if any, that can stand to have their private lives scrutinized without embarrassment. Changing societal norms can render previous social media posts harmful to reputations, especially if the individual develops a desire for public office.

Beyond their impact on identity and privacy, social networks warrant three other considerations:

## 1. Surveillance

The social networks themselves may not have much interest in the interactions, search histories and digital conversations of individual users, but other parties might, including the authorities. All organizations, including governments, perform surveillance of some kind – be it watching over property, employees or citizens – to make sure rules are respected and safety is preserved. In constitutional democracies, there are limits to the surveillance that can be conducted, unless legally authorized and based on reasonable grounds. Is this enough to reassure us that personal history held by social networks will not be tapped into by government agencies? History would suggest otherwise.

The East German government was notorious for its surveillance efforts. By 1989, the East German Ministry for State Security (the Stasi) employed 91,015 full-time staff and maintained 173,000 paid informants overseeing a population of 16.4 million people[40] – one informant for every sixty-two people in the country. Surveillance concerns are not restricted to totalitarian administrations, however. In the United States in 1928, bootlegger Roy "Big Boy" Olmstead was indicted on the strength of evidence collected using multiple wiretaps executed without warrants. Olmstead's appeal, based on Fourth Amendment rights, went to the Supreme Court. Federal prosecutors argued that wiretapping did not constitute physical trespass and that telephone conversations were not strictly private, as they involved two parties and the phone company. Olmstead's conviction was upheld and wiretapping continued to be done without a warrant for most of that century. It was not until 1967, in *Katz v. United States*, that a court held that wiretapping without a warrant, regardless of no physical trespass taking place, was unconstitutional per se and reversed the previous ruling.

One government argument against privacy rests on the need for early detection of terrorist and criminal activity – perhaps an uncontroversial goal at first glance, but one which merits further scrutiny. Governments of every political stripe seek to engineer the values and behaviours of the societies they govern. Societies, meanwhile, evolve, and when the evolution does not align with the government's aims, there is conflict. The government may take steps to supress behaviour deemed illegal or antisocial, while reformers will try to change governing laws and policy. Time and again, we've seen that driving societal change requires privacy, since fledgling organizations can be snuffed out by surveillance from government agencies. As Lawrence Cappello has observed, "When people are aware that they are being watched, they tend to alter their behaviour to fit what they believe to be general expectations of 'normal behaviour' so as not to draw attention to themselves."[41]

While there is little risk that social networks will use data against their subscribers, governments – acting with or without warrants – may sift through personal contacts, search histories and posted opinions looking for signs of activity they may consider questionable, if not necessarily criminal. Police need a warrant to gather personal information from an individual, but information voluntarily provided to another party is not similarly protected and can be obtained with a court order served on the service provider. Social networks, therefore, open the door to levels of surveillance far greater than those enabled by wiretaps or physical observation. Users should be aware and take precautions.

## 2. Fair Value for Information Provided

In 2022, the market capitalization of Meta, the parent company of Facebook, was US$552 billion, while the market capitalization of Alphabet, Google's parent company, was US$1.3 trillion. Monetizing personal information is lucrative.

Whenever personal information is gathered, the question arises of what can or should be revealed, and to whom. Similarly, there is the question of what can or should be concealed, and from whom. In some relationships, multiple parties have access to information; the question then is who can be permitted to use the information and for what purpose.

When shopping online, both the retailer and the customer have the customer's browsing history and purchases. Does either own this information? Can either party use this information however they wish? The answers to such questions can depend on regional privacy laws, but the general principle is that each party can use the information to enhance the relationship between the parties. The retailer can use browsing and purchase history to suggest additional products and services, solicit feedback or build marketing models. The shopper can post information about their experiences. The retailer cannot sell the information to other marketing organizations unless express consent is collected from the shopper. (This also holds true for social networks, financial institutions and telecom providers.) The retailer cannot alert government authorities, the individual's employer or their insurance provider of the shopper's purchases, for example, if they were buying firearms, alcohol or medication.

Can any party with access to information collect consent from the individual to make their information available to other parties? The answer is yes, but they must be explicit in how the information will be used and for how long it will be retained. Even with such consent, privacy officers have concerns about the imbalance of power between the party collecting the information and the individual providing it, as people generally have little understanding of their data's commercial value. This allows social networks to ask for, and receive, access to personal information for commercial applications while offering little in return – for example, building powerful advertising and marketing businesses while offering users free content.

## 3. Security

In addition to well-publicized hacks and data breaches, there have been instances when information in the hands of social networks has not always been protected. In 2022, Facebook notified roughly one million account holders that their accounts may have been compromised by malicious apps able to steal their login information.[42] If these users were logging in to other accounts with their Facebook credentials, even more of their information would have been exposed.

Social networks maintain secure systems and take steps to protect account holder data. They regularly monitor and test their networks, follow information security policies and implement access control measures. They protect their reputation. Exposure of account holder information does not have a direct impact on their ability to deliver advertising services, but poor security erodes public trust, reducing usage and advertising reach. So far, the networks have been reasonably resilient to security incidents.

The Cambridge Analytica scandal of 2016 is a well-documented example of a social network's failure to protect account holder information and its consequences. In 2014, Global Science Research paid users to take a psychological test using an app called "thisisyourdigitallife." The app not only gathered information on those taking the test but also on their Facebook friends. While this was a violation of Facebook's policies, it was not detected or prevented, and up to 87 million Facebook profiles were mined for data and then sold to Cambridge Analytica for targeting pro-Trump messaging during the 2016 American presidential election.

The UK Information Commissioner's Office investigation of the incident led to more than a year of litigation and appeals, after which Facebook agreed to pay a fine of US$643,000, the maximum that could be levied under the UK *Data Protection*

*Act* of 1998. New data protection laws passed in 2018 have since increased the maximum fine to US$22 million.[43]

Facebook made no admission of liability but announced changes to its platform and imposed tighter controls on the information app developers could access. While there was public concern, with some Facebook users declaring an intention to abandon the platform, the concern was short-lived, and Facebook recovered from the scandal.

Marketing based on customer information is not new – businesses have been direct marketing since catalogues were first printed and offers could be mailed. American Express built a direct-marketing business that presented customers with offers based on purchase histories; speciality magazines sold subscriber information to create prospect lists for target marketing. While yesterday's databases were limited to names, addresses and phone numbers – crudely sorted by area of interest – the scale and range of data collection and marketing in the digital age has changed the game. As Joseph Stalin said, "Quantity has a quality all its own." It has never been as easy or inexpensive to collect and store personal information, but the legitimate marketing that it powers is not the reason to be concerned about social media.

Though privacy concerns first arose over publication of photographs, most people now willingly share and promote their photographs, inviting others to like and subscribe. We grew up with phone books providing names, addresses and phone numbers of entire populations – information now considered private – yet an online search of a name, or even an image, can identify people and tell you more about them than ever before. So long as knowledge-based questions and anecdotal information continue to play a role in identity verification, information derived from social media has the potential to do harm. Fortunately, these forms of verification are being phased out – replaced by multifactor authentication, biometrics and hard credentials – but though these improved verification tools may put an end to social media's contribution to identity theft, the privacy concerns remain. With the continuing evolution of social norms and expectations, whatever we say, do and post today may look very different to people twenty or thirty years from now, with the potential to come back to haunt us. Living in the digital world leaves a record that will be stored and remain available, either openly or through hacking, breaches, warrants or subpoenas. Information about us will be collected, stored and used by the global digital advertising industry; privacy laws will be of little help if people keep trading away rights for convenience. The only way to deal with these concerns is through education and awareness, which will inevitably occur as new generations growing up in the digital world replace those still struggling to understand its implications.

# 6 Big Brother is Watching

The way things are supposed to work is that we're supposed to know virtually everything about what they [the
government] do: that's why they're called public servants.
They're supposed to know virtually nothing about what
we do: that's why we're called private individuals.

Glenn Greenwald, American lawyer

THE AUSTRALIAN GOVERNMENT HAS STUDIED digital identity and
made efforts to implement personal digital identity credentials. In
*Preventing Another Australia Card Fail: Unlocking the Potential of
Digital Identity*, Fergus Hanson, head of the Australian Strategic
Policy Institute, describes how the Australian government oper-
ates more than thirty different logins for online services; a digital
identity program could deliver reductions in cost and fraud,
improve customer experience and save the Australian government
$11 billion annually.[44] He cites government estimates of $17 to $20
for verification each time an Australian tries to prove their identity to access a service online, while the cost of doing this digitally
would be between $0.40 and $2.00.[45]

A national multi-purpose digital identity program could enable millions of real-world transactions to move online; enable easy delegation of authority, such as picking up prescriptions or medical test results; and facilitate privacy-respecting verifications, such as demonstrating proof of age without revealing name and address. Governments across the globe hunger for such attractive benefits, and some countries are already starting to implement government-issued digital credentials.

What is a national digital identity and what would a program delivering one look like? How would this be different from using our existing government-issued credentials online? While there are different ideas being considered, most programs have three common elements:

- A central authority operating a hub with access to databases managed by government agencies

- Strong authentication to verify the identity of the applicant

- An app with a secure credential on the applicant's mobile phone

With a national digital system in place, an enterprise would not need to independently verify a driver's licence or any other identity credential provided as proof of identity by an individual. The individual would instead grant permission for a central authority to provide (or verify) their driver's licence, and the central authority would release (or authenticate) the credential for the requesting party.

This idea has many attractive features. First, it follows best practices for handling personal information, allowing for only required information to be released. Today, when a driver's licence is used as proof of age, the applicant also reveals their birthdate and address, neither of which is actually required if a reliable yes or no answer to the proof-of-age question could be returned. Second, the central authority would notify the individual every time any of their personal information was accessed; for example, if a fraudster applied for a credit card using a stolen identity, the victim would be alerted by the central authority once it received the verification request. Only the central authority would have access to government databases (reducing the likelihood of hacking or unauthorized access), and no new databases containing personal information would be required (minimizing the number of places personal information is stored).

Delivery of a national digital identity program is a significant undertaking, but the required technology is available. Considering the significant benefits of such a program, why aren't we seeing more implementations? Governments already enable security, trade, currency, social programs, transportation, communication and other essentials of daily life with their services. As interaction moves to digital channels, it would seem only natural for governments to take a greater role in digital authentication. After all, we have a government-issued driver's licence, health card and passport, so why not go further with a new online identity credential?

National digital identity programs face two serious challenges: one is related to implementation; the other to public acceptance.

Implementation is challenged by the complexity of dealing with multiple levels of government as well as different government organizations, information systems and legal requirements. Each organization is mindful of protecting the personal information under its control. Orchestrating responsibilities and costs across levels of government and different departments does not come easily or naturally, and there's little incentive for any party to move the program forward as the benefits will not necessarily accrue to the parties enabling the service. Moreover, budgets across the board are tight, with little room to embark on large new projects that promise returns in the distant future. This challenge, daunting though it may be, could be overcome with effort and coordination;

getting the public to accept an identity program that would give the government access to everyone's online activity, however, is more difficult.

In the *New Yorker* article "Why Do We Care So Much About Privacy?" Harvard University Professor Louis Menand writes, "The government is doing what it has always done, which is to conduct surveillance of individuals and groups it suspects of presenting a danger to society. And commercial media are doing what they have always done, which is to use consumer information to sell advertising ... What makes us feel powerless today is the scale."[46]

A centralized authority governing digital identity would have access to all personal information and online activity. This could be available to law enforcement authorities and other government agencies. It would be of great interest to commercial enterprises building attribute profiles of consumers and would give significant power to anyone with access to the data. Errors in the system would disrupt the lives of individuals, and experience shows they would be hard to correct. All of this means that widespread concerns over how information would be used stand in the way of adoption – without which there would be no benefits.

Both history and fiction provide examples of dystopian government identity and surveillance programs. George Orwell's *1984* gave us "Big Brother is watching you" – a theme that has resurfaced in numerous books and films. Franz Kafka gave us stories of omnipotent bureaucracies creating nightmarish worlds for individuals powerless to correct erroneous accusations. With a digital identity program able to make either of these a reality, would the public endorse it?

Jon Agar, Professor of Science and Technology at University College London, has studied government initiatives with identity cards. The scale of hostilities during the First World War demanded total mobilization of Great Britain's industrial capacity and human resources. The need to know the number of people available for industrial and military purposes prompted legislation for a national register in 1915, which contained the names and addresses of all persons between the ages of fifteen and sixty-five, allowing each to be issued an identity card, which was signed and retained. If an individual moved or if a card was lost, local registration authorities were to be informed so that records would remain reliable.

The national register was not a success, and it was abandoned after the war. Despite public support for the war effort, there was little enthusiasm for the formalities required to maintain the register, little understanding of its significance and no sense of personal benefit.

The British identity card of the First World War had a quiet death, and a nearly forgotten grave. The movement of people and the loss of cards led to numerous applications for new cards from the citizenry, but new cards were often not matched to old cards. The rapid growth in number of records in the National Register caused by this process of "inflation" led to the system becoming first unwieldly and later useless. [47]

Despite the military's desire for national registration after the war, a peacetime register was considered impractical. With the onset of the Second World War, civil servants were tasked with making identity cards more valuable to the public so this tool of wartime administration could function more effectively than it did during its previous incarnation. National registration, with identity cards, was introduced for the second time as a foundation for food rationing, although it would also be used for the other purposes previously envisioned. The register maintained information on individuals such as age, gender, marital status and participation in national service, and in addition to assigning ration books, the card acted as proof of identity to apply for a passport, open a bank account and retrieve a parcel from the post office.

The usefulness of the cards compelled people to look after them, and this time, national records were maintained. Identity cards were a fact of life during the war, with police officers routinely asking the public to produce them. As food rationing was slowly phased out after the war, resentment began to build towards a practice that came to be seen as bureaucratic bullying. Newspapers wrote anti-card editorials, such as that published in the *Daily Express*: "Except as a wartime measure the system is intolerable. It is un-British ... It turns every village policeman into a Gestapo agent."[48]

In 1950, Clarence Willcock was stopped in his car by a police officer who asked him to show his identity card. Clarence refused, arguing that the *National Registration Act* ended when the war finished. In the widely publicized court case that followed, Willcock was found guilty but given an absolute discharge. Willcock, emerging in the press as a local hero fighting for individual liberties, appealed the decision before the King's Bench Divisional Court in January 1951. Although his appeal was rejected, the court approved of the absolute discharge Willcock was granted. In his concluding remarks, the presiding judge wrote:

> To demand registration cards of all and sundry – from a lady leaving her car outside a shop longer than she should for instance – is wholly unreasonable ... We have always prided ourselves on the good feeling between the police and public, but this tends to make people resent the acts of the police, to obstruct instead of assist them.[49]

Public support for the British identity card system continued to decline, and the program was again abandoned within a year of the *Willcock v. Muckle* decision.

Is government oversight any more accepted today than it was in Great Britain after the Second World War? Without near-universal public acceptance of a national identity system, it's doubtful whether the surveillance and bureaucratic effort required to enforce and maintain the system in a top-down manner would be any more acceptable today. Even if supported and well maintained, the system would do little to eliminate fraud. Because all British citizens were entitled to an identity card, it was possible to obtain one without much scrutiny – a problem facing all programs that must be available to all members of society – which made the system ripe for misuse. Stolen identity cards could be presented for extra ration books, and no solution was found to prevent the use of supplementary or fictitious identities. Once an identity card was issued, it was generally accepted as a government endorsement, and a fraudster could use it with impunity. The only thing authorities could do was increase scrutiny and surveillance, which further added to public resentment.

Most people's first identity document is a birth certificate establishing when and where they were born. This becomes the foundation for other documents, such as a passport or driver's licence. While a birth certificate is good evidence that a birth occurred, was documented and was recorded, it's harder to prove its link to a specific individual after the fact, leading to birth certificate fraud.

In a September 2000 report on birth certificate fraud in the United States, the Office of the Inspector General documented the major contributors to this type of fraud and concluded, in summary, that birth certificates are easy to obtain and hard to verify.[50] Because over 6,000 entities in the United States were able to issue birth certificates using different materials and formats, distinguishing between a legitimate certificate and a fraudulent one was difficult. Some offices issued certificates on security paper; others didn't. There was no consistency in the use of serial numbers, latent images, ultraviolet ink, hidden voids, security threads and other features. Periodic changes to formats, and the fact that certificates had no expiry dates, added to the number of different versions in circulation.

The report listed 6,422 birth certificate–issuing entities in the United States, including those at state, county, city and township locations. Fourteen states allowed open access to birth records, meaning that anyone could review birth records or purchase a copy of a birth certificate if they knew the name and birthdate of the person on the certificate. Thirty-six states restricted access to birth records, meaning that only the person listed on the birth certificate or their designated representative could obtain a certified copy; however, only nineteen of these states required proof of identification for walk-in requests, and just eleven required it for requests by mail. For proof of identification, many registrars said they would accept any documentation with a control number, including employment badges, library cards, bus passes and utility bills.

Did birth certificates get issued to fraudsters? The Office of the Inspector General reported that 90 percent of the false claim cases detected by an El Paso intelligence center involved genuine birth certificates held by imposters.[51] The US passport office similarly reported that 85 percent of their birth certificate fraud was perpetrated by imposters using genuine, government-issued birth certificates. Once imposters were issued with a birth certificate, they could apply for other documents to build their fraudulent identities.

David Shearer, a professor of twentieth-century European history at the University of Delaware, has studied government initiatives related to identity. Governments document and monitor identity, he writes, for controlling movement; mobilizing economic resources, such as taxation; managing benefits for citizens; and for reasons of security or repression.[52] In most democratic countries, governments need to maintain records of their citizens for two reasons:

- To ensure people fulfil civic and personal responsibilities – with taxation being the most prominent but not only example

- To ensure people exercising privileges are entitled to do so – for example, confirming an individual is entitled to drive, vote, access health care or attend a school

Information technology has enabled government agencies in the United States to store and share information about the lives of Americans since the 1960s. Concern over privacy rights led to Congress passing the *Privacy Act* in 1974, but technology was changing rapidly and personal privacy was difficult to define with any precision. This left room for creative data mining, which led, in some cases, to unintended and horrifyingly unjust outcomes. In the 1970s, government investigators were able to cross-reference data on federal employees against lists of recipients of welfare benefits to find what were all believed to be a host of fraudulent irregularities, which led to both savings and prosecutions.

The process, however, was crudely executed – it also unearthed irregularities that were not associated with fraud. Some were the result of mistaken identity or coding errors, while others could be accounted for by special circumstances, such as the adoption of a child with a physical impairment. As a result, thousands of innocent Americans were subjected to wrongful arrest, termination of employment and refusal of medical benefits.[53] Despite that, data mining was promoted as a way to reduce waste and fraud, and between 1980 and 1984, federal and state agencies conducted over 533 computer matches looking for irregularities associated with over seven billion individual records.[54]

Another example of a government seeking to identify, categorize and monitor its citizens was the internal passport system implemented in the Soviet Union in the 1930s. Established to itemize the population and associate individuals with a residence and place of work, it reduced the population from a complex mass of individuals to a range of simplified types subject to government control over movement, access to resources and even liberty, through involuntary exile to labour camps.[55] The passport defined each individual by occupation, ethnicity, social status and history of interaction with the authorities. Passports were registered with local or regional police offices, and movement required an individual to deregister at one office and reregister at a new one. Police were quick to take advantage of the system and used it to carry out sweeps of everyone fitting a profile when pursuing an individual.

Despite potential concerns, governments around the globe are exploring digital ID systems. The United Kingdom is developing a smartphone and website digital ID with the aim of making digital passports and licences as reliable as their physical counterparts. Digital ID will not be mandatory; people will have the option of continuing to use their physical credentials. France enacted the Digital Identity Guarantee Service into law on April 26, 2022, a smartphone-based extension of France's national identity card. This smartphone app allows the phone's NFC capability to read the chip on the identity card and prompts the user to enter a PIN to authenticate themselves. The German government is developing a similar program that will use a smartphone app with NFC capability to read a national ID card and store the information on the phone as an electronic ID (eID). The plan is for eIDs to eventually enable access to over 575 government services, including voting in public elections.

China has a digital ID program with a national ID card, as well as a social credit system. The national ID card builds on digital ID cards that have been issued in major cities since 2018, extending coverage across the country. The social credit system is an attempt to gauge an individual's trustworthiness, taking a traditional financial credit score and either lowering it, should the individual be associated with non-financial social actions such as corruption, tax evasion, academic plagiarism, counterfeiting or pollution, or raising it, in the case of blood donation, charitable work, cultural achievement or athletic accomplishment. There have been reports of the social credit system being used to punish those who recycled incorrectly or neglected to wear masks during the COVID-19 pandemic.

The Western world is built on a foundation of personal freedom and democracy dating back to Aristotle, who maintained that "the basis of a democratic state is liberty," a view echoed in present times by Dr. Ann Cavoukian, former Information and Privacy Commissioner of Ontario and leading privacy advocate. She wrote, "The most innovative societies also happen to be the most free and privacy protective. Freedom and privacy form the foundation, the very bedrock, of innovation."[56]

Citizens of Western democracies expect freedom from surveillance and undue search. Personal property and information are considered private, unless authorities can build a case for lawful access. Static credentials, such as passports and driver's licences, do not enable ongoing surveillance. In the digital world, however, everything can be tracked. A personal digital identity would allow online activity to be monitored in real-time or viewed by anyone with system access – and people are right to be concerned about the resulting unintended consequences. As nineteenth-century British politician Lord Acton once wrote, "Power tends to corrupt, and absolute power corrupts absolutely."

Anyone familiar with the digital world knows that much of what we do is already tracked: Google has our search history, Apple has the online activity of its customers, Amazon has our shopping history, our internet service providers know the websites we visit, and mobile network providers know our location. We can take some comfort from the fact that we freely choose to deal with each of these companies and could end these relationships if they misused our information. There's also comfort in knowing that companies are not only legally bound by privacy laws, but protecting information also aligns with their business interests. When the US National Security Agency was unable to unlock a suspect's iPhone, Apple refused the FBI's request to assist them on the grounds that doing so would harm its business.[57] Government agencies have no access to information collected by private firms unless granted by the courts. On March 1, 2024, in a 5 to 4 decision, the Canadian Supreme Court ruled that police need a judge's authorization to access Canadians' IP addresses, confirming that online activity is protected from warrantless searches.

If government agencies were managing digital authentication, they could have direct access to our online lives with unlimited capacity to screen for fraudulent, antisocial, criminal or questionable behaviour. We've seen authorities access data for these purposes in the past, making it unlikely that there will be enough public trust for this to happen in the foreseeable future.

As for the trustworthiness of credentials, so long as governments feel the need to provide universal access to services, verification systems for confirming identity will continue to be undermined. The stories of Great Britain's national registry and US birth certificates show that genuine government credentials can, and do, end up in the hands of fraudsters. Would a new program be any less susceptible to fraud if it had to be made available to everyone?

Despite these concerns, the benefits of a national digital identity cannot be ignored. Most people alive today are likely to experience some form of a government-sanctioned system that will follow a gradual, evolutionary path and aim to leave control of personal information in the hands of individuals. Separating service delivery from government scrutiny will be important for public acceptance, and education will be needed for people to manage their digital identities effectively. Questions and concerns over privacy and security will persist and hopefully lead to an outcome that respects individual privacy and liberty – but it's unlikely to be more secure or trustworthy than the digital credentials available today.

# 7 Saved by a Treefort

The irony is that cattle are actually pretty good at finding the path of least resistance, which is often the best route for a road.

Karin T. Wood, "Pave the Cow's Path"

IN THE IT WORLD, THE phrase "paving the cow path" can be used as a put-down of people who automate a process without first optimizing it. Of course, if you maintain a process, it does avoid the problems that come with change management, and it can make adoption of the automated solution faster. Can identity verification be accomplished in a similar way by digitizing existing practices from the real-world? Treefort Technologies shows us cases where this is possible.

Jay Krushell grew up in rural Alberta, Canada, where as a child, he built a massive tree fort from discarded barn lumber on his family farm.[58] As a young man, he earned degrees in communication and business administration, completed a law degree and then embarked on a career in commercial law. While law was his profession, he remained driven to find new challenges and ways to overcome them. For a while, he satisfied this drive with mountain biking, marathons and ultramarathons. But after nineteen long-distance races, Jay felt his athletic pursuits were not meeting an intrinsic need, which he realized was a desire to bring new solutions and services to the business world. When his law office lost important clients in 2013 because of the time it took to execute files, he saw the loss as an opportunity. Focusing on the root cause of the problem, he set out to fix it, creating a software platform he called Lending Assist to reduce the time spent on document processing and due diligence search. Lending Assist proved very effective – it could accelerate file processing by up to seven days. This led to the formation of Lending Assist as a software company, with Jay's wife, former Edmonton city councillor Kim Krushell, as president. Jay's software solution met with strong market acceptance, and with investment from private equity and another legal software firm, the service expanded across Canada and the United States.

As he continued in his law practice, Jay grew increasingly frustrated with another problem: uncertainty in identity verification within commercial lending. Lawyers are routinely involved in transactions with significant financial implications, such as those in real estate or business, but they aren't held to the same standards of customer verification required by financial institutions. This has made Canadian lawyers targets for money laundering and fraud, a point highlighted by the international Financial Action Task Force. When Canadian authorities tried to hold the legal industry to verification and reporting requirements similar to those imposed by FINTRAC, law societies resisted, citing principles of solicitor–client privilege, and their arguments prevailed. Nevertheless, all parties recognized the problem and agreed that something had to be done. The law societies and federal authorities continued to work together, reaching an understanding that would require lawyers to verify identities but maintain the confidentiality of client accounts. The realization that changes would be coming to identity verification in the legal profession just magnified Jay's interest in the challenge.

He set about trying to find ways to bring the legal profession's identity practices into the new millennium. Armed with an idea and a plan, he assembled a team of tech professionals and formed Treefort Technologies in 2020 – naming the company after his childhood tree fort. His goal was to provide lawyers with identity verification tools strong enough to reduce the potential for crime in high-value transactions.

While many assets are at risk of being stolen, you might think that at least your house would be safe. That is not the case. Fraudsters have been known to use one set of fake ID to rent a property and a separate fake ID to pose as the home's owner, and then successfully list the property for sale or use it to secure a mortgage loan. All of this can often be accomplished with little more than a fake driver's licence. Lawyers typically require clients to present themselves in person for identity verification, but that adds cost and complexity to transactions involving clients who either travel or are located elsewhere.

Lawyers must, and do, ask clients to present identity credentials; in some cases, they also perform a credit check. They try to assess the authenticity of the documents presented and judge whether or not the client is their rightful owner. Jay had learned that "fraudsters adeptly exploit false identities when using driver's licenses to bypass existing safeguards – deceiving realtors, lenders and lawyers. To combat this problem, Treefort developed multifactor authentication technology that goes beyond just looking at government-issued ID to confirm the identity of an individual."[59]

Jay set out to integrate multiple verification methods into a single service that would be better than the digital equivalent of the in-person process used by lawyers. While the tech industry was already making digital verification methods available, they were not easy to use and all came with some challenges. Some required end-user registration, others were expensive, and still more came with concerns over privacy and the storage of the customer's personal information. Jay felt a web-enabled service to which lawyers, real estate agents and land transfer insurers could invite clients to verify themselves would provide the industry with safe and convenient identity assurance. Consistency and convenience would help cut through the clutter of different verification methods, accelerating customer education and acceptance.

There were already suppliers offering the ability to assess a scanned document for authenticity and test whether the image matched a selfie sent from a smartphone. Aiming for a level of verification that would meet the standard for financial institutions, Jay layered on additional sources and services to enhance security, such as checking that the mobile account belonged to the client and for evidence of a bank account. These were packaged into one full-service identity verification platform.

In 2020, Treefort introduced identity verification for lawyers, real estate agents and land transfer agents. This is how the process works. The relying party – the lawyer or agent dealing with a customer – is Treefort's client. The relying party tells their customer to expect an email requesting identity verification. They then send their customer a link to Treefort's service, which is supported by a code sent to the customer's mobile phone. This code allows for two-factor authentication of the customer's identity. The customer must review and accept Treefort's privacy terms and conditions before they can proceed with the ID verification process. Using their cell phone, the customer is asked to upload their ID documents – a driver's licence, passport or both – followed by a selfie, with liveness detection, to ensure the person matches the image on the documents. A firm specializing in document verification and image matching analyzes the information to make sure the photos match the face scan and the documents are authentic, with no signs of fraud or tampering.

Behind the scenes, Treefort verifies the information provided with a credit bureau, a bank and the client's mobile service provider. The credit bureau performs an automated verification of the client's name, address and date of birth, as well as a credit score. Bank account information further verifies the account holder's identity and provides the tenure of the account; the mobile service provider confirms the mobile number is registered to that user, and also confirms the type and tenure of the mobile account. If the mobile device shows signs of tampering, such as a SIM swap or recent number port; if the mobile account is an anonymous prepaid account, or burner phone; or if the account has only very recently been established, then additional verification steps are needed to confirm the customer's identity. Experience has shown that fraudsters invariably use anonymous prepaid accounts or contract accounts recently established with false names.

The process generates a report that incorporates over one hundred data points, analyzes the customer's identity and assesses fraud risk. It is sent to the relying party, together with copies of the information collected during the evaluation.

The multiple sources provide strong verification. The credit file and bank account help confirm that there is a real person linked to the identity, not a fictitious one. Confirming the person is in possession of the device associated with their mobile number offers reassurance that the person providing the information is the named individual, not someone using stolen information. Checking the documents for authenticity and matching the image to the selfie helps discourage fraudsters from submitting forged documents. While the availability of high-quality forgeries makes it difficult to guarantee that documents are authentic, this last check raises the bar for fraudsters trying to leverage stolen credentials.

But, as we've seen elsewhere, developing a promising solution is only part of the battle; getting adoption in a field as fragmented and diverse as law and real estate can be more challenging than developing the solution. Fortunately, Jay and Kim were both well connected and skilled in communications and market development. They started working their contacts in provincial law associations and approached companies in the title insurance industry – the latter being important stakeholders, since they are the ones suffering the loss if the homeowner is insured.

In 2023, the Canadian Broadcasting Corporation (CBC) reported that organized crime groups were responsible for over thirty homes being sold or mortgaged in the Greater Toronto Area without the real owners' knowledge, with identity theft instrumental to the sale of the properties.[60] Homeowners with title insurance are protected from both financial losses and the legal expenses to re-establish their title rights, and a buyer purchasing the fraudulently listed home is also protected, helping them get their money back. John Rider, a senior vice-president at the Chicago Title Insurance Company of Canada, told the CBC that the number of claims had grown from near zero to dozens in just a few years. "There's four title companies in the business in Canada and we estimate that industry wide, it's easily $200 million, probably more, in fraud claims in the last two-and-a-half years."[61]

One of Canada's title insurance companies, Stewart Title Insurance, took notice of the Treefort solution, saw its possibilities and invested in Treefort. In the press release, Marco Polsinelli, president of Stewart Title's Canadian division stated:

> Stewart Title invested in Treefort Technologies because we believe its IDV tool is thorough and reliable. Since most fraudulent real estate deals involve impersonation, using it has helped us and our clients prevent millions of dollars in potentially fraudulent transactions. By offering Treefort to their customers, LTSA [Land Title and Survey Authority of British Columbia] has added another tool in fighting title

fraud and safeguarding Canadian customers and the integrity of our real estate system as a whole.[62]

Stewart Title went on to purchase a 51 percent interest in Treefort Technologies and used their majority stake to appoint Grant Goldrich, a thirty-year veteran in services supporting business transactions and regulatory compliance, as Treefort's new president. This gave Treefort access to new sales channels for identity verification in legal, real estate and title insurance offices across the nation.

While still in the early stages of the adoption cycle, the Treefort service is being used in transactions by three of Canada's four title insurance companies. It's also starting to be adopted by law offices across the land, a trend that may be accelerated by recent regulatory requirements.

In 2020, the pandemic curtailed in-person interaction in the legal profession, as it did in many other businesses. Provincial law societies put emergency measures in place that relaxed identity verification requirements and allowed clients to verify identity online by presenting credentials during a video call. Law offices discovered that this was not only a convenience for clients, but it also allowed them to extend their market coverage beyond their local areas. When law societies tried to retire the emergency measures in 2022, lawyers objected, and the term for relaxed requirements was further extended. To allow lawyers to keep their online clients while bringing the period of relaxed verification to an end, law societies are setting more rigorous digital verification standards. These new standards will likely increase demand for identity verification services and suppliers such as Treefort.

But no one in the industry is expecting change to happen overnight. Despite this support for online verification, lawyers are notoriously conservative and often technology averse. Digitizing identity verification throughout the legal profession may take some time; policy changes that require more stringent verification will help accelerate the process.

Nonetheless, what Jay and Kim at Treefort have shown is that following the path of least resistance can lead to a successful outcome and paving it will help everyone get there faster.

# 8 The SecureKey Solution

The goal of the project was ... to prove that we could actually solve the problem, that we could have citizens show up, be able to share their data in a privacy-enhanced way, be able to get services more expeditiously and have less fraud.

Greg Wolfond, CEO of SecureKey Technologies

GREG WOLFOND HAS ENOUGH ACCOMPLISHMENTS to fill two lifetimes. As an entrepreneur, he has led a series of start-ups that have realized business success, earning him recognition as Canada's Top 40 Under 40, Entrepreneur of the Year and one of the Top 100 Leaders in Identity. Alongside that, he raised a family and found time for cycling, running and triathlons. When a relative of Greg's had his identity stolen by a fraudster who used it to take out a $100,000 mortgage loan on his house, Greg decided to take action. Around the time of this incident, in the early 2000s, identity theft was already a global concern, and fraud was on the rise. In this case, the fraudster seemed credible: he presented forged but convincing documentation, the named individual's credit rating was good and the house had more than enough equity to justify the loan. To the bank, the transaction did not seem like it deserved much scrutiny, and the fraudster made off with $100,000. To Greg, there were too many of these kinds of fraud cases, given there were measures that could be put in place to prevent them. Not one to think small, he set his sights on a global solution.

Back in the 1990s, well before anyone spoke of the "internet of things," Greg thought he might want to do his banking on a Nintendo machine.[63] He partnered with a lawyer who had a background in computer engineering as well as an electrical engineer to form 724 Solutions, which provided wireless infrastructure and software to enable mobile banking, brokerage and e-commerce. 724 Solutions grew to count the Bank of Montreal, the Bank of America and Citigroup among its clients, and when the company went public in 2000, it was one of the most anticipated stock launches of the year.

For Greg, lightning had struck a second time. He had already seen success as the founder of Footprint Software, a developer of object-oriented technology for financial applications. Its flagship product, Visual Banker, received international recognition for bank branch automation, and the company was acquired by IBM in 1995 for $50 million.

As Greg turned his thinking to identity theft, his background in software and banking systems provided insight into how banks verified identity and authorized account access. He knew that advances in chip and PIN technology were virtually eliminating credit card fraud at retail points of sale. If "what you have," in the form of a chip-enabled card, and "what you know," in the form of a PIN or password, could verify identity for retail payments, why couldn't the same approach be used to verify identity everywhere?

Could all internet connected devices, laptops and phones, be equipped with the same type of secure cryptography used by chip-enabled cards, and could these credentials be linked to verified identities? If this were possible, then every device that was matched with a personal PIN could be used to reliably identify its user. This, of course, was easier said than done, but Greg set out to find a way to do it.

A global solution needs global reach, and this is best achieved with partners, so he started by explaining his vision to the parties that could help realize it. At the time, Intel produced the vast majority of chips used in connected devices and could equip these chips with the needed cryptography. The credit card companies were already authenticating chip and PIN cards and could provide the needed authentication. Greg formed a new company, SecureKey Technologies, with partners that included Intel, Visa, Mastercard and Discover. Staffed with a handful of engineers and programmers, SecureKey started work on an application that would allow any device to reliably verify its user. Since computers were not yet equipped with the necessary chips, the SecureKey prototype put the technology on a USB key that could be plugged into a computer. Each USB key had a unique identification chip and an NFC antenna; the chip enabled identification, and the antenna enabled it to interact with contactless cards.

Once SecureKey's USB key was inserted into a computer's port, it enabled the computer to present the identity credential stored on the key. Moreover, the NFC antenna on the key allowed it to function as a bank card or payment card reader, meaning people could present cards for online verification by tapping them on the USB key, like at a retail payment terminal. An online shopper, for example, could tap their card on the USB key, add their PIN and have their credential verified by the card network before a transaction was sent to a financial institution for approval. The ability to present cards during online shopping would transform card-not-present transactions, making payment fraud significantly more difficult.

Impressive though this was, the world was not yet ready for it. People were unlikely to embrace USB keys for logging in to websites, and retailers were unwilling to risk the loss of sales by demanding that cards be presented. For mass adoption, the technology had to be built into computers and phones. The cryptography would add about a dollar to the cost of each Intel chip, and Intel wouldn't do it unless device manufacturers paid the extra cost. The hardware market, however, was intensely competitive, and manufacturers wouldn't accept the extra cost without evidence of market demand. Development hit a dead end. Without a viable product, the outlook for SecureKey's future in identity verification was beginning to look doubtful. Greg needed to find something with immediate potential for the company to survive.

The online industry was having a problem with password resets. People were able to manage their passwords for regularly used accounts, but many forgot or misplaced their passwords for accounts they rarely used. The Canadian income tax authority, Revenue Canada, had a very secure but cumbersome process for enabling online access to accounts. To open an online account, the individual had to demonstrate ownership of their tax file by providing specific information from previous tax filings. To ensure security, Revenue Canada would mail the requesting party a one-time access code to the residential address on file. This access code was needed to create an account, after which the account owner could establish a password. Inevitably, the next tax season, many people were unable to remember or locate their passwords, with many unwilling to go through the account-creation process again. Password resets were a costly customer service issue for Revenue Canada.

Could SecureKey's identity verification technology help solve Revenue Canada's password problem? The idea, eventually called SecureKey Concierge, was to allow people to reuse their bank login as authentication for Revenue Canada. Rather than set up another unique username and password, a person could link their bank credential and password to their tax account. Revenue

Canada would check with the bank to ensure that the combination of username and password was valid, confirming it was the same customer – which would then let people use login credentials they were unlikely to forget to access their Revenue Canada accounts. But once again, this was easier said than done.

Banks go to great lengths to protect their client information and credentials. They have always been careful to ensure that login credentials are never used anywhere except the bank's login page, which helps reduce the risk of people using their credentials on sites controlled by fraudsters. Banks would, therefore, not allow their credentials to be input into a Revenue Canada site; the client would have to be redirected to a bank site for verification to take place. While this added some complexity, SecureKey set out to make it manageable.

To use SecureKey Concierge, a client still had to authenticate themselves to Revenue Canada, as they had before, and receive a one-time passcode to create an account. Once the account was established, however, they didn't have to create a new password; instead, they could link their Revenue Canada account to the bank account of their choice. Revenue Canada would redirect them to their bank's login page, where they would input their username and password. Once the bank verified the login and authorized account access, the bank provided an authorization token that SecureKey sent to Revenue Canada. This linked the client's tax account to the client's banking credentials, so the next time the client wanted to log in to their Revenue Canada account, they could choose to log in through their bank. Revenue Canada would redirect them to their bank's login page, where they would submit their credentials for authorization; once approved, Revenue Canada would again receive the authorization token from the bank by way of Securekey. In this way, the client could access their Revenue Canada account.

The solution was elegant, efficient and secure, although people had to be educated on how to use it. Some were afraid that logging in with a bank password would give Revenue Canada access to their bank accounts, which was not the case; Revenue Canada never saw the login credentials, nor did they see whose bank account was being used or even which bank provided the verification. The solution only gave Revenue Canada the assurance that a bank considered the username and password combination valid, with the bank satisfied that it was for the same client. This allowed Revenue Canada to benefit from the many authentication measures that banks had developed to recognize and verify returning clients. The solution was very client friendly, since people logged in to their bank accounts, on average, three times each week and were unlikely to forget their bank passwords.

Despite its elegance, the solution would remain on the drawing board unless all the parties involved agreed to do the development needed to make it work. Banks would have to implement connections to SecureKey, and Revenue Canada would have to build a link enabling logins through SecureKey's hub. Asking any bank's technology department to verify a login for a third party was like asking an aircraft carrier to deliver a parcel: it could do it, but it would only agree to do so if there was no change to its existing course or mission. SecureKey had to prove to the banks that it would do all the customization required to integrate bank services into the solution, that there was no security risk to bank systems and that the verification service would make a positive contribution to bank clients' experiences. Initially, three banks agreed to support the development of SecureKey Concierge, but by the time the service launched in 2012, all of Canada's major national financial institutions were supporting the solution. The service proved a huge success, and was soon used by over eighty Government of Canada agencies and more than 10 million Canadians.

The technology SecureKey developed to enable a USB attachment to read bank cards was spun off into a separate company and sold. The solution was eventually incorporated into Square, a plug-in device that allows merchants to use phones and tablets as payment card terminals, and which is now used by over 24 million clients.

Strictly speaking, SecureKey Concierge provides authorization, not identity verification; it gave SecureKey a commercial service and way to stay in business, but it didn't help verify identity. But Greg knew the components he needed for an identity solution were now available. He conceived of a comprehensive verification application called Verified.Me, a smartphone app that could provide identity verification, account access and secure delivery of personal information to relying parties. During registration, an individual's identity would be verified using SecureKey's ability to log in to a bank account. The mobile number of the individual's device would be verified by the serving telco, and the name checked against the telco's records for that mobile account; this would bind the phone's SIM card to the Verified.Me account, giving each account a secure, hardware-backed identifier. Together with a PIN, this would combine "what I have" with "what I know" for online verification. SecureKey's management of the app would not only provide ongoing security through a distributed data base of information shared across networks, but it would also enable connections to other databases, allowing the person registering for the app to authorize relying parties to access personal information stored by other parties.

The vision was powerful. A person could check their credit rating, authorize access to their driver's licence or use their banking information to open a new financial services account, all with verified personal information. In addition, they could identify themselves to access health records or apply for new government services, and it would be equally effective for online and in-person interactions. There was even a viable business model to support the service, by charging the relying party a small fee for information received or identities verified. The fee would be shared with the information provider, creating an incentive for parties to join the program.

Leveraging bank and telco records provided strong verification. Banks already had to satisfy regulatory requirements for customer verification; the addition of telco services helped weed out those using synthetic or stolen identities. Fraudsters did not normally go to the trouble and expense of maintaining a wireless account to support a false identity, and both banks and telcos could monitor accounts and identify those with unusual activity. Having an identity verified against a known account with regular activity significantly reduced the likelihood that someone was not who they said they were. Tying the service to a unique device reduced the opportunity for sophisticated fraudsters to use digital impersonations of voices or images, or forged documents. The Verified. Me technology offered many significant benefits, but once again, adoption would prove challenging.

Getting people to download the app presented the first conundrum. Until a sufficient number of devices were enabled with the service, online enterprises would not do the work required to make use of Verified.Me; however, until there were places where the app could be used, people would not download the app and register. At the time, app marketplaces were exploding, and companies were providing incentives to encourage downloads of their own applications, but there was no financial model to support the incentives needed to encourage downloads of Verified.Me.

Another challenge was the complexity of the system SecureKey was trying to build – a novel distributed ledger or "blockchain" technology that could authorize access to existing databases for identity verification. SecureKey's objective was honourable, perhaps even altruistic; once an identity was verified, enterprises and clients could continue on with business between themselves as before. Yet to some, it looked like SecureKey was trying to set itself up as an authorization or authentication gateway that could collect information on people's online activity, like a social network. However, the SecureKey network was triple blind – no party, including SecureKey, knew who was accessing information or who was providing it. But doubts about future intentions persisted, which made some enterprises hesitant to connect.

Another concern was that SecureKey was still a small private company. Would banks, governments and major enterprises be comfortable making critical platforms rely on services from a business with an uncertain future?

Verified.Me launched in May 2019, twelve years after SecureKey was established, with seven major financial institutions enabling access to their client information for identity verification. Identity could not only be verified, but name and address information could be provided to fill in the forms for those applying for new accounts. Soon after launch, the service added a document scanning and verification capability with facial recognition. The service was enabled through any web browser, eliminating the need for an app. All requirements were in place for secure verification and a user-friendly experience.

A person applying for a credit card online with a bank that was served by Verified.Me would have the option of clicking the Verified.Me icon to start the process. This would redirect them to their own bank's login page, where they would log in as usual and consent to having their information provided for the application. The application form would be prefilled with their name, address and contact information. The bank receiving the credit card application would have the assurance of knowing that they were dealing with a real, verified person whose identity had been checked by the bank providing the information. All in all, it was an elegant solution.

A year after launch, however, SecureKey was having a hard time building a user base. Few relying parties were set up to use Verified.Me for account creation, and most of the banks that supplied data for the service had not yet undertaken the work to enable it for establishing new accounts.

The pandemic had driven banks to find alternatives to relying on branches for opening new accounts. Banks were investing in digital channels for new applications, and most had already developed some way to carry out identity verification online. Some chose the FINTRAC dual source method, using a credit bureau as well as document scanning combined with photo recognition. Some banks partnered with Canada Post, which provided identity verification in person at its post office locations.

Within a bank, the responsibility for identity verification could be distributed across multiple functions, including compliance (for anti-money laundering and know-your-customer requirements), fraud management, cybercrime, digital channels, marketing and individual business functions. To justify investment in a new verification service, the bank required a business case showing that the benefits would offset the costs. With benefits being uncertain and distributed across numerous teams or departments, the business case was hard to prove.

It was also difficult to find an advocate to champion the service. The most powerful internal voice is usually the business leader responsible for bringing in new clients. The failure rate for activating new clients online was high – often around 50 percent – as clients either failed the verification requirements or abandoned the process partway through. Since banks were already using credit bureaus, new clients with valid credit bureau files did not usually fail. Since anyone with a bank account had a credit bureau file, candidates who could use Verified.Me were already passing – so adding the service would not lift the success rate.

SecureKey tried to engage the telcos to use Verified.Me for account creation. At the time, telcos relied on retail outlets for most of their new clients, with identity checks conducted in person; moreover, telco fraud losses were relatively small. With many other projects competing for scarce development resources, it was once again hard to prove a business case for using the service.

But, there were opportunities for online identity verification and authorization in health care, education, voting, insurance, law and government services. The Digital ID and Authentication Council of Canada (DIACC) estimated that reliable digital identity verification could save small and medium businesses in Canada $4.5 billion annually, in total, up to one percent of Canada's GDP, or $15 billion.[64] SecureKey became a strong and visible advocate for a national digital identity infrastructure; its employees spoke at conferences, published position papers and participated in the DIACC. While there were numerous opportunities to use Verified. Me to enhance security, each implementation was complex, often costly, and frequently required extensive customer education and support. Verified.Me had launched, but building a community of users was more difficult than expected.

Canadian banks had helped build SecureKey's identity service, and it still played a part as banking services evolved, such as open banking (consumers sharing financial data with third-party providers) and real-time payments. Eventually, it was felt that identity verification was too important to leave in the hands of a tech startup; the banks wanted more control.

Then Interac showed interest in SecureKey. Interac is a financial network that was formed by Canada's major financial institutions in 1984 to help manage cash dispensing through automated banking machines. It has grown into a trusted financial brand whose services include debit payments, e-transfers and, most recently, digital ID. Interac has connections to every financial institution in Canada, takes direction from a board with representation from these institutions and is consistently ranked as one of the nation's most trusted brands. Seeking growth opportunities and recognizing that the technologies supporting payments and identity were closely intertwined, Interac turned its attention to identity verification. Combining SecureKey's technology with Interac's distribution and brand could deliver benefits to both organizations; it would also give the banks more control over the future of Verified.Me in Canada. On October 1, 2021, Interac announced that it was acquiring exclusive rights to SecureKey's digital ID services for Canada.

Greg was still pursuing a global vision for identity verification and actively building partnerships in global markets, including the United States, Australia and Europe. Giving Interac exclusive rights to SecureKey's services in Canada allowed Interac's market reach and brand trust to help drive adoption of SecureKey's solutions domestically – but it didn't help with the global reach.

The Interac news, it turned out, did not go unnoticed. Less than six months after the Interac announcement, SecureKey was approached by a global technology company that issued the following press release on March 24, 2022:

> Avast (LSE:AVST), a global leader in digital security and privacy, today announced the acquisition of SecureKey Technologies, a global provider of digital identity and authentication solutions headquartered in Canada. SecureKey's next generation privacy-enhancing services are focused on simplifying access to online services while giving control back to consumers by ensuring the information they share with others is only ever with their explicit consent.
>
> Identity and Authentication and reusable digital identity services are expected to grow to $266bn by 2027 with a CAGR of 68.9%, according to Liminal (formerly OWI), the digital identity specialists, with the private sector to capture

the majority of this growth. SecureKey's mission has been to simplify consumer access to secure online services and applications, such as government, healthcare and financial account opening, utilizing secure digital versions of the credentials they already have and trust.[65]

With new owners in control, Greg Wolfond retired from SecureKey at the end of 2022. Verifying digital identity remains a challenge, but his efforts have created a suite of verification technologies and a foundation for identity verification that could one day be expanded across the globe. Greg remains convinced that SecureKey's technology can deliver the solution to online identity verification, although he recognizes that it will take some time. Scanning a driver's licence and matching the photo to one's image may be part of an identity claim, but it presents a low bar for fraudsters. Not only will fraudsters have the digital tools to spoof credentials and images, they've shown they can get their hands on genuine, government-issued identity credentials. The problems associated with issuing credentials to the right people and revoking them if they fall into the wrong hands are not easily solved. However, since banks are motivated to protect the security of their accounts, demonstrating the ability to log in to a bank account provides substantial proof of identity. Banks maintain state-of-the-art verification methods that recognize devices and usage patterns, help identify unusual activity and weed out imposters. Banks have deployed multi-factor authentication, incorporated device-based biometrics and used services that highlight unusual patterns of behaviour. So long as these services remain effective in verifying bank clients, identities verified by Verified.Me can also be trusted.

Yet, like any difficult sales proposition, until (or unless) much of the population adopts the Verified.Me service, it will remain an overlay to the other verification methods used by an enterprise.

So long as less effective verification methods are supported, doors remain open to fraudsters. There is also the "chicken and egg" problem of users not wanting to engage with a service until there are places to use it, and enterprises not wanting to invest in a service until there are users. It's not an easy service for an enterprise to pilot, nor is it an easy service to explain to the public.

Nevertheless, much of what Greg envisaged for SecureKey is coming to pass, albeit slowly and, so far, only in selected applications. Apple products have evolved to have secure credentials that allow Apple to definitively identify devices and verify users. This capability helps secure Apple's payment service, and it's starting to be used for third-party identity verification. As of 2024, four states (Arizona, Colorado, Georgia and Maryland) have introduced digital driver's licences, and Apple has enabled the addition of digital driver's licences to the Apple Wallet. Using a hardware credential to verify identity will become more important with the growth of new artificial intelligence (AI)–driven abilities, which help fraudsters make digital copies of credentials, images and even biometrics. Generative AI can already simulate images and voices using relatively small samples, which may be indistinguishable from their authentic counterparts.

The benefits of the SecureKey solution remain as relevant as the day they were conceived. With Verified.Me (now called Interac Verified in Canada), no new tracking credential is created that could lead to an erosion of personal privacy, and there's no new honeypot of personal data to act as a target for hackers. The service also leverages a credential that banks must continue to protect and keep secure; nevertheless, it remains one approach among many looking for adoption in identity verification. Only time will tell whether its compelling features will be enough to lift it into the mainstream, or if it will remain a point solution.

So far, however, it hasn't paid to bet against the eventual success of Greg Wolfond's new ventures.

# 9 Bluink and the Identity Wallet

A good scientist is a person with original ideas. A good engineer is a person who makes a design that works with as few original ideas as possible.

Freeman Dyson, theoretical physicist
and mathematician

STEVE BORZA, EVER THE CONSUMMATE engineer, has three decades of experience in identity, access control and biometrics. In 1999, his "biometrically secured control system for preventing the unauthorized use of a vehicle" was granted a patent,[66] but the use of technology similar to his facial recognition system is only now seeing early stage trials in the automotive industry – proof that Steve can be ahead of the curve.

Steve is the president of Bluink, a company that has developed an identity verification and digital identity service that uses the smartphone as a strong authenticator and secure digital identity wallet. Confronted with the challenges of verifying identity online, Steve created a workable solution, but once again, he may have to wait for the world to be ready for it.

Steve is a hands-on engineer. He personally designs and builds products, as well as the production lines that manufacture them. In the 1990s, he was at American Biometric, where he created the BioMouse Plus, the world's first integrated smartcard and fingerprint scanner that enabled three-factor authentication for secure logins to a computer. The device used "something you are," "something you have" and "something you know" in the form of a fingerprint, a smartcard and a PIN or password. The product was designed for enterprise clients requiring high security, especially where computers had multiple users. The first customer was the Chase Manhattan Bank, but other clients soon included JP Morgan, Microsoft and the US Department of Defense, with the product used by the military in Operation Desert Storm. American Biometric designed and manufactured a variety of access control devices and was ultimately acquired by ActiveCard in 2001. By then, Steve had left to join another start-up in optical electronics, a field attracting significant investment at the time. He then worked at a couple of security and encryption–related technology firms before creating Bluink as a technology and research consultancy in 2010. As was typical for Steve, the firm was soon developing new products.

Steve envisioned a password manager that stored encrypted passwords on a smartphone, making them available for accessing websites on a computer via a Bluetooth connection; the passwords could be backed up to other devices or controlled as to where and how they could be used. It was a service similar to the Apple Keychain (which also manages passwords and information), except the passwords were stored locally on the smartphone instead of in the cloud. While a number of technology firms expressed interest in the service, Steve found that, once again, it was too early for general deployment.

In 2015, while showcasing Bluink's capabilities at Identity North, a Canadian conference designed to help develop the identity management ecosystem in Canada, Steve met a representative of Ontario's provincial government who expressed interest in his password manager as a tool for identity verification. Bluink was granted a development contract to create an identity wallet, which led Steve to design eID-Me, an app that could securely store government-issued credentials on a smartphone for presenting in person or online. The provincial government had designs on its own identity service, but the government was voted out of office at the next election, killing the project. Fortunately for Bluink, a number of corporate clients saw potential for the service, with some interested in "white label" versions of eID-Me (rebranded to the company) for their own digital platforms. These contracts, together with the original development contract and some new private funding, were able to keep Bluink going. Finally, eID-Me was introduced into the Apple and Google app stores as a stand-alone application that could digitize government-issued credentials and store them on a mobile phone to be either viewed or transmitted to another party. The fact that eID-Me credentials are not considered legally acceptable as authentic, government-issued credentials has not stopped some parties from accepting them when presented. Three layers of technology support eID-Me: one that verifies the documents as they are loaded into the app, one that securely stores the documents on the phone and one that securely presents them to relying parties online.

As with many identity services, the initial verification of identity during the application process is the crucial step, for which the app uses a multi-tiered solution. As documents are scanned for storage in the app, machine intelligence checks the documents for authenticity and any signs of tampering. One piece of government-issued ID must bear the individual's home address, and registration must be done at home, as the app will match the phone's location at the time of registration with the residential address on the credential. The person must also use the camera on the phone to take a guided selfie video that checks for liveness and confirms that the image matches the photo on the ID.

When the app was launched, it was able to scan and verify Canadian driver's licences from every province, passports, Nexus cards, permanent residency cards and Secure Certificate of Indian Status cards. Passports incorporate a chip that can be scanned directly by an NFC-enabled smartphone, further reducing the opportunity for document tampering. Additional documents can further confirm identity and increase the usefulness of the app for the user by making the documents available for future reference and presentation.

Encryption is used to ensure that the credentials are secure when stored on the phone; they are decrypted when the app is unlocked using the phone's biometrics (face or fingerprint ID). The app is connected to a server that provides the encryption keys to unlock the credentials. To receive eID-Me credentials online, the relying party must be connected to and authenticated by the eID-Me server; the owner of the credentials must also authorize the relying party to receive them. This gives the individual full control over their personal information. Credentials are never exposed over the internet.

Steve introduced eID-Me in March 2020 during an identity conference in Washington, DC, and garnered interest from government and enterprise clients. Unfortunately, the conference came to an abrupt end after its first day due to lockdowns imposed because of COVID-19. In spite of the constrained business environment, Bluink continued to make progress with clients. Canada Post was looking for ways to strengthen the security of its services to ensure only authorized people could redirect mail or receive updates on deliveries. It already offered identity verification for third parties through its retail locations and selected eID-Me to help extend its identity verification capability online. A white-labelled version of eID-Me in the Canada Post app would allow for persistent, secure storage of credentials that could be reused to prove identity as required. The eID-Me service has many strengths. It securely stores personal identity information on an individual's smartphone so no new database of identity information is created for hackers to attack. Information is not released, or even accessible, unless the individual provides authorization – personal data is never released without consent. Access to the wallet is protected by the phone's biometrics, providing a high level of assurance that only the authorized user can use the service. Bluink's server monitors both the app and requesting parties to ensure that only verified parties are connected to the service. The end-to-end process is all done using machine-to-machine connections, with no personal data ever made available to individuals. This makes the service both privacy-enhancing and readily scalable for wide adoption. Finally, people seem to be able to complete the onboarding process successfully; Bluink reports that over 75 percent of applicants successfully download and register their eID-Me wallets on their own or with the aid of online resources. The success rate jumps to 95 percent once live assistance from a help desk is provided.

As Steve acknowledges, document scanning combined with facial photo matching can be spoofed by resourceful fraudsters. Relying on this alone provides a relatively low level of assurance – identity assurance level one. When a passport is added to the wallet by having the passport chip scanned, the level of assurance is enhanced to level two. The passport chip is encrypted, but it can be unlocked by reading the machine-readable zone, a standardized code at the bottom of the passport ID page. The app can verify that the passport information was collected from the original passport chip, the passport was issued by the country of origin, the data were digitally signed, and the digital signatures of all the data align and have not been tampered with. Steve believes this offers the best form of digital identity verification available globally, and over 150 countries now issue chip-enabled passports. So far, no fraudster has overcome Bluink's security measures, and Steve is confident he can keep them at bay. To him, the bigger problem is fraudsters continuing to get their hands on authentic, government-issued driver's licences and other credentials to create digital identity wallets. Fraudsters have succeeded in getting other people's driver's licences issued to them with their own photographs; people have also lost a driver's licence while travelling and had a replacement sent to a foreign address with little authentication. Unless fraud can be controlled at the source, no level of security at Bluink will be able to completely eliminate the use of eID-Me by fraudsters.

Enterprises that need reliable customer verification online have taken an interest in Bluink's technology. A law firm has started using eID-Me for real estate transactions, and a national security organization is using it for background screening services and criminal record checks. Getting governments to accept eID-Me for proof of identity, however, will be crucial for widespread acceptance; Steve is counting on the successful execution of several government contracts to achieve this. This includes identity verification within various levels of government for government contractors, government employees and citizens accessing public services. As with other verification services, the business model will require the relying party to pay a small verification fee that will be shared to create a revenue stream for the information provider. This may one day even allow individuals to collect revenue from making their information available for identity verification, encouraging the adoption of verification services.

To no one's surprise, the wheels of government services turn slowly. There are also plenty of skeptics who feel the public will refuse to use government-enabled digital credentials for fear of surveillance and concerns over privacy, though Steve remains optimistic that acceptance will come with time. "Young people understand that they are tracked. If you are on Twitter or TikTok, you're tracked. They are pretty much over that, and they want convenience. They ask 'Why can't I use my phone?'"

Visionary business leaders aim to steer the market to where they want to go. There are also business leaders that study the market to see where it's going and try to get out ahead, anticipating the products and services that the market will need – Steve is that kind of leader. His detailed knowledge of international standards bodies, technical specifications and government initiatives is helping him prepare a smartphone-based digital identity technology that government programs will need once they're ready to embrace digital identity credentials. He may, once again, be well out in front of the curve.

Steve remains confident that digital credentials, generated from their physical counterparts and stored in phones, are the way of the future; he expects that driver's licences will be the first to appear in our mobile wallets. It has taken about a decade, but the International Organization for Standardization, headquartered in Geneva, Switzerland, has issued ISO/IEC 18013-5, the technical specification for a mobile driver's licence. Mobile driver's licences are already available in several American states. Passports, health cards and other credentials are eventually expected to follow, and standards for some have already been developed. Government credentials issued with chips will be securely loadable into digital identity wallets, such as eID-Me, where they can be used for in-person and online presentation. Undoubtedly, this will be slow to launch; implementation requires evaluation of competing standards and alignment of policies across different levels of government. Even within individual levels of government, there are differences of opinion between functional departments and digital service architects. Many standards bodies and corporate interests are involved, with competitive lobbying for specific implementations.

In the end, global adoption may not hinge on the efforts of governments or standards bodies but may boil down to how Apple, Google, Microsoft and IBM align on implementation. They are, after all, best positioned to reach, educate and influence large numbers of end-users, both citizens and enterprises.

# 10 The Problem is Choice

Choice is an illusion created between those with power and those without.

Merovingian, *The Matrix Reloaded*

BEFORE YOU COULD TAKE YOUR iPhone anywhere on the planet and expect it to work, mobile phones came in a range of technologies, each tailored to the network to which it would connect: AMPS, NAMPS, TACS, NMT, TDMA, CDMA and others were all in service, and all incompatible. At one time, three different digital technologies were in use in Canada alone. Luckily, in little more than a decade, the wireless industry moved to a single standard, Global System for Mobiles (GSM), allowing handsets and networks to be able to exchange and use information everywhere. The move to a standard did not deny consumers choice – there were still multiple handset manufacturers and mobile network operators from which to choose – but it eliminated the need to match handsets with serving networks, ending considerable frustration. Network operators also welcomed it, since it eliminated the need to make high stakes technology decisions, reducing the likelihood of being left with network equipment unsupported by popular handset manufacturers. An industry that fragments into different technologies forces both suppliers and customers to make choices that can reduce options rather than increase them – as anyone who recalls the Betamax versus VHS battle in video standards can attest. A single standard supported by multiple vendors offers customers the most choice.

Treefort, SecureKey and Bluink each developed different approaches for verifying identity online. Customers comfortable with one of them would not necessarily feel the same about the others. Given the many other verification technologies under development, the industry is likely headed for a period of fragmentation. The global market for identity verification can certainly support scores of suppliers, even different technologies, but a standard approach has significant benefits. A standard prevents the frustration that arises when a client equipped with one verification method is faced with a company set up for another. Different and evolving coexisting solutions make it harder to distinguish between legitimate credential requests and fake ones aimed at stealing personal information. A standard helps accelerate adoption among enterprises by reducing the risk of investing in a solution that might see little uptake among users or could be abandoned and no longer supported by its supplier. Most of all, a standard would reduce the need for customer education and support by ensuring that all verification services worked the same way.

While standardization, or even alignment around a smaller number of solutions, would simplify deployment and accelerate uptake, there is the risk that it could lead to concentrated control over personal information or easier access for unauthorized monitoring of online activity. Standards also create winners and losers among solution providers, with those adopted as standard having the most to gain – "winner takes all" or "winner takes most."

It's too early to say which, if any, approach in development can rise to the level of a global standard, but a similar saga, already played out in mobile payments, offers some lessons. Less than twenty years ago, non-cash payments were carried out exclusively by payment cards. As cards gained complexity, with added microprocessors and radio frequency identification antennas, it became apparent that what they did could also be done by smartphones. What the phones lacked was a personalized credential that identified the card user and their account. Such credentials were put onto chips at a factory, attached to plastic cards and delivered to the account holders; however, if instead they could be securely delivered to the phone over the air, could plastic cards be rendered obsolete? We once put movies on plastic discs and sent them through the mail; that stopped with transmission over the air and the internet. Could the same work for payment cards?

A payment card has a few essential components: personalized credentials unique to the user and their account, credentials specifying the brand and type of card, a chip with encrypted information that can be read by a card terminal, and a loop antenna embedded in the card to allow data transmission wirelessly. Most banks rely on card manufacturers to produce their cards and issue them to their clients under the bank's direction. The market is concentrated among a relatively small number of companies (such as G&D, Oberthur, Morpho, Gemalto/Thales), which also, coincidentally, produce the SIM cards for the wireless industry – the chip in a payment card is in fact identical to the chip in a phone.

To put a card in the hands of a bank customer, the bank specifies the card type, assigns a client account and securely transmits to the card manufacturer. Card production is carried out in high-security facilities of the kind that also print currency and produce government documents, such as passports. Entry to the facility can require a retina scan, with visitors weighed as they enter and exit to ensure that nothing leaves with them. Once the card is produced, it is delivered to the client in an unmarked envelope to avoid attention during transit.

Transmitting the card and account information to a secure storage space in a smartphone could reduce time, cost and risk, but it would still require high security, encryption capabilities and the ability to manage information on secure storage chips. The potential benefits attracted interest from many parties, including banks, mobile network operators, card associations, and card and smartphone manufacturers, who all made efforts to establish themselves as channels for delivering payment credentials to smartphones – and this set the stage for fragmentation.

Lessons were learned from the rush to deploy multiple over-the-air credential delivery platforms by different suppliers. Despite attempts to align on industry standards, there were differences in operating systems across SIM card manufacturers, security requirements across card associations, smartphone operating systems and their different versions, and bank card issuing systems, where each bank had proprietary customizations. When a bank created, delivered and operated its own payment app, clients with payment credentials from other banks found that their phone's antenna could lock onto one credential and not release it for use by another. Minor differences in credential formatting could prevent a card from being accepted by a phone's operating system, so failure rates for card delivery were high. High failure rates when presenting credentials at retail terminals forced each bank into extensive testing across different devices and terminals to make sure their services worked. Frustration levels were high among consumers and industry participants alike, with deployment costs rising and customer adoption falling below expectations.

Then, in 2014, Apple announced Apple Pay, which was first introduced in the United States. It was supported by Visa, Mastercard, Amex and six major banks representing 83 percent of the US card-issuing market. Apple provided the secure element chip in the phone for payment credentials and also operated the secure element management system delivering the credentials to the chip. The card associations – Visa, Mastercard and Amex – tokenized the cards and delivered their tokens to the Apple Wallet in a consistent, standardized manner. Customers were presented with a very user-friendly application for loading, managing and accessing their cards, while banks could leverage their existing connections to Visa, Mastercard and Amex to enable mobile payments for their clients. By designing an end-to-end system with standardized tokens mapped back to card accounts, taking control of token delivery and managing the tokens on the phone, Apple eliminated the complexity that was causing problems in the ecosystem.

At first, banks were outraged at the prospect of Apple inserting itself between them and their customers; after all, they had made significant investments in their own credential delivery services. Banks also took offence at Apple's demand for a percentage of the banks' payment fees in return for providing the service. Despite their misgivings and initial refusal to deal with Apple, the banks began to realize that it would be more expensive and less effective to continue with the solutions they were developing than it would be to use Apple Pay. Even though, at the time, Apple Pay addressed only half the market in North America and still less globally, one by one the banks, card manufacturers and mobile operators threw in the towel and wound down their efforts. Apple Pay, followed in 2015 by Android Pay (now Google Pay) and Samsung Pay, emerged as the platforms for payment credentials on smartphones. When customers selected a smartphone, they defaulted to a mobile payment service; by integrating the service into their operating systems, the tech companies improved reliability, security and customer experience. The choice of mobile payment service, once thought important, fell by the wayside.

Both mobile payments and digital identity require high security, robust reliability and tight integration of different and complicated systems. In both cases, members of the ecosystem don't fully trust each other and harbour legitimate concerns that profit margins or customer information could be usurped by others. This makes it hard to have a smoothly running, efficient and customer-friendly multi-party service; the parties all incur costs and customers experience frustrations while inefficiencies are ironed out, which slows adoption. Market participants looking for a return on investment eventually come to question the commitment of the additional resources required before success is realized.

In this type of environment, a well-resourced enterprise that takes a long-term view has a significant advantage – and this is especially true if it also has a large and loyal customer base. Apple entered the mobile payments market knowing that it would take ten to fifteen years to see a return; it also had the tools, technology and brand strength to design a service that could delight customers. If it so chooses, it could do the same for identity. Identity verification would add value to Apple's products so the company wouldn't need to drive a new revenue stream from the service, making it difficult for stand-alone service suppliers to compete. If Apple clients have the option of using an Apple identity wallet, competing services will have a tough time gaining traction on Apple's platform. To some extent, the same would be true on the Android platform should Google offer an identity wallet, although Google has not shown Apple's level of commitment to personal privacy.

Apple, notoriously secretive about product strategy, will not disclose its plans for digital identity, but we can look at what the company has already done. Apple was a participant in the development of ISO 18013-5, the international standard for mobile driver's licences, and it has developed a service using that standard. On September 1, 2021, Apple announced it was working with several states to enable driver's licences and state ID cards to be added to the Apple Wallet. Arizona was the first to make the service available, with Colorado and Maryland following. States issuing digital credentials still require physical versions to be carried, and the digital versions may not be honoured outside the issuing state. In spite of this, the Transportation Security Administration has confirmed that digital credentials are acceptable at airport security checkpoints, and by 2024, four US airports were equipped to accept them.

The process for adding credentials to the wallet resembles that for adding payment cards. The individual enters their licence or ID number, scans the card and takes a selfie with movement for liveness detection. The request is sent to the issuing state for verification, after which, the credential is added to the wallet. Once added, the credential resides in the smartphone under the owner's control and is no longer accessible by the issuing state.

According to Apple, the service offers better security and privacy than a physical wallet. Customer information is encrypted and only accessible when unlocked by the owner using the smartphone's biometric authentication capabilities. As with physical credentials, neither Apple nor the issuing state can see if, when or where credentials are used. If the device is lost, the owner can remotely lock it or erase it – security measures that are impossible with a physical wallet. Another benefit is that when using an identity reader, only the requested information is presented, and then only with the owner's consent. Providing this information does not require the owner to unlock or present the device to an official to verify their identity.

While Apple's efforts always attract public attention, other digital ID initiatives are also in progress. Google is developing similar functions for the Google Wallet, and several states are working with technology companies to develop their own apps for storing digital IDs, some of which have so far chosen not to enable their credentials on either the Apple or Google wallet.

Will Apple and Google emerge as the leaders in mobile ID as they did in mobile payments? They do start with some advantages. Since they control the iPhone and Android operating systems, they can preload the software for their identity wallets and ensure that system updates do not affect authentication or require re-registration. Since Apple designs and manufactures their phones, they have ways to enhance security that are not available to third parties; this includes using the phone-based hardware secure element to store credentials, keeping credentials safe from hackers and malware, and keeping information private. Google also has a "trusted execution environment," a storage space in the software of the operating system that offers similar benefits. Neither can be accessed by third-party applications without Apple's or Google's permission. Perhaps most importantly, they can also securely manage clients through migrations to new devices. When you get a new iPhone, Apple can authenticate you on your other Apple devices and move your functionality to the new phone. A third-party identity wallet, copied onto a new device, can appear suspicious to the wallet supplier, which may then require either re-authentication or a new download of the original credentials.

Identity credentials also have some important differences from payment credentials. Many are government issued, and governments want to control credential distribution and use. They have requirements that the tech companies may find difficult to accommodate, including domestic control over data processing, inspection rights and lawful intercept (legally sanctioned access to private communications). These alone could keep Apple and Google from connecting to government credential issuers in some jurisdictions. Governments also like to promote customer choice and may request that tech companies grant competing identity service providers equal access to smartphone features, something not normally granted to third-party payment services for security and customer experience reasons. Finally, many governments aim to make services available to the entire population. This would be an advantage for third-party identity wallets where a single connection could enable service across both Android and Apple platforms. In all likelihood, governments will try to create ecosystems that could be served by multiple suppliers, but that would not prevent Apple or Google from being among the most popular or successful of the mobile ID services.

# 11  The Road Ahead

Trust those who seek the truth but doubt those who
say they have found it.

André Gide, French author and Nobel Laureate

WHEN THE DISCIPLES TOLD THOMAS they had seen the Lord, he
said to them, "Unless I see in his hands the mark of the nails, and
place my finger into the mark of the nails, and place my hand into
his side, I will never believe."[67] Just like Thomas, we can only be
certain of the identities of people we know well and only when we
meet them in person. Without a reliable method for online identity verification, we are left managing levels of assurance and risk.

Identity professionals talk about four levels of identity assurance, with increasing confidence from level one to level four. There
is some variation among interpretations of the four levels, but they
all require an increase in the amount of information collected in
order to ascend the levels. Level one requires only self-assertion;
you don't need to provide any evidence. For example, a name and
email address are enough to request an online newsletter, create a
free email account or register an account on a website. Level one
creates an identifier that allows a party to track an individual, but

any association with an identity is loose at best and should not be trusted.

Level two requires one piece of evidence that can be verified with an authority. This could be a credit card verified by the issuer, a driver's licence, or a mobile number verified by the network provider. Examples requiring level two include booking a hotel room, making a secured restaurant reservation or opening an online account with a utility. Level two provides an identity, but it offers little confirmation that the person using the identity is who they say they are.

Level three requires two verified pieces of evidence, with one being from a government source or financial institution. In addition to requiring verification of the information provided, level three calls for confirmation using an out-of-band channel, such as a one-time passcode sent to the applicant's mobile number or email address to verify the contact information. At level three, the applicant is linked to the account with a biometric, knowledge-based question, physical credential or third-party confirmation. Level three is required, for example, when you open a bank account or apply for a credit card.

Level four requires rigorous verification of the applicant's identity, with some assurance that the applicant is the person providing the information. Individual policies may introduce some differences in the process, such as asking for four pieces of evidence matched to the individual, with confirmation of each piece of evidence from its source. In some cases, in-person verification may be required. Level four calls for the same out-of-band linkage of the account to the individual specified in level three. Level four is needed, for example, for passport applications and will be required to allow transactions that now can only be done in person to be carried out online.

Stepping up verification from level one to level four is largely a difference in degree rather than kind. Apart from adding muti-factor authentication or requesting an in-person meeting, the relying party must still assess information that has been input, scanned or photographed. While the information can be verified against other databases, there is no guarantee that the person named in the application is the person making the request. Even at the highest levels of assurance, an online "doubting Thomas" would not be satisfied. Databases of personal information can be hacked, passwords phished, accounts hijacked and two-factor authentication thwarted, while increasingly sophisticated software now even mimics images and voices. While it may be impossible to guarantee an identity online, higher levels of assurance significantly reduce risk and deny fraudsters easy returns.

Accounts protected by only a username and password remain soft targets for fraudsters – with hacks, breaches or phishing serving up the necessary access credentials. Phishing attacks are easy and inexpensive, and can be automated and scaled to deploy in large numbers. Fraudsters launching millions of attacks need only tiny success rates to realize meaningful returns. The best recourse, of course, is to never click on unsolicited links, but even the wary can be swept up by the urgency of a request or an unexpected angle. Managing multiple online relationships makes it challenging to separate legitimate requests from fraudulent ones – and the occasional misstep is hard to avoid. The attacks continue to be run because they work.

Fraudsters also enjoy a structural advantage. Enterprises are responsible for confirming the identity of clients, but they don't have full control over the process. Effective identity verification uses an ecosystem to coordinate the interaction of service suppliers, intermediaries, relying parties and the general population. Not only does establishing this take time, but education is required before improvements are effective. Criminals, however, are not so constrained. They work independently, moving quickly to deploy new methods of attack and novel ways to trick victims into surrendering personal information. A lack of customer education works to their advantage. The fact that enterprises take different approaches to verifying identity further muddies the water, since being confronted by different and changing verification demands makes it even harder for people to separate legitimate requests from fraudulent ones. With just a superficial understanding of the ways identity is managed, most people have little appreciation of the risks they take when cutting corners for convenience – a condition exploited by fraudsters.

Despite the many service offerings available from technical and commercial suppliers, no market has yet seen widespread adoption of a single solution for identity verification. As we've seen, the reasons for this are many: concerns over privacy and security, fear of concentrating too much information with a central authority, the complexity of different systems and a reluctance to bear the added cost. The market is looking for convenience and security, but investors backing suppliers are looking for a return. The global identity and access management market was valued at over US$15 billion in 2022 and is projected to grow by more than 12 percent annually until 2030.[68] Many continue to believe that identity management will be dominated by a small number of large suppliers, which offers up the prospect of a lucrative "winner takes all" or "winner takes most" opportunity to those who can crack the code. So far, the prize remains unclaimed, but it's not for lack of effort.

The story of ZenKey shows how hard it is to succeed in this market. The major US telcos – AT&T, T-Mobile and Verizon – recognized that fraud and identity theft were growing problems in the digital economy. They also realized that people needed consistent and standardized tools if they were to learn to manage their online identities. With 90 million account holders across the three telcos, they launched a joint venture to deliver identity verification as a service in the United States. Founded in 2019 and headquartered in Atlanta, Georgia, ZenKey was announced by the US telcos at the Mobile World Congress in Los Angeles in October of that year. It started work on an effective, full-service identity management service using telco resources, with phones and SIM cards as the hardware tokens anchoring the identity of individual clients. People would manage their digital identities using the ZenKey app, which was designed as a digital identity wallet; passports and driver's licences could be scanned, checked for authenticity, compared to selfies enabled with liveness checks and stored in the wallet. Enterprises that enabled account creation using ZenKey could have client information prepopulated and subsequent logins authenticated; this would also give users the ability to securely log in to multiple sites with a single password, eliminating password management headaches. The carriers would monitor connections for real-time fraud indicators, such as SIM swaps, call and message redirection, and suspicious activity from short-tenured accounts. Individual users would be provided with a summary of their online activities and allowed to manage access rights granted to their personal information.

ZenKey's strengths did not stop with strong authentication, identity proofing, ID validation and online fraud detection; it had the financial backing of the telcos and access to telco sales channels. The latter would be important in addressing opportunities that ZenKey envisaged in workforce and government markets.

ZenKey's goals were ambitious, but it had the assets, resources and financing to realize them. The app was launched in September 2020 – but just three years later, the telcos pulled the plug.

What went wrong? Telcos are good at managing major capital projects and large customer bases, but the telco industry is now focused on delivering earnings. New business cases need to show a payback, often in less than two years. ZenKey was dependent on verification services for revenue, but deploying and supporting services was costly and revenue was slow to build. There were also no services for which using ZenKey's authentication was essential, so customers saw no compelling need or urgency for the service. Since few people had downloaded the app and registered for a ZenKey identity wallet, relying parties had little incentive to add ZenKey as an enrolment or login option. Not wishing to alienate their subscribers, the carriers themselves did not insist that they use it. ZenKey had counted on traffic from major online players like Amazon and Netflix, but it could offer little beyond what was already available from established single sign-on services from Google or Apple. Given enough time and funding, ZenKey may have been able to build a base of clients and end-users big enough to break even, but it was off to a slow start and unlikely to generate the returns demanded by the telco owners. Once AT&T, T-Mobile and Verizon realized this, they cut their losses and abandoned ship.

While ZenKey shows it's not easy to build an identity verification service, it doesn't mean that it's impossible. There are paths that can lead to success – unfortunately none of them were open to ZenKey. Meanwhile, other investors and entrepreneurs continue to seek global identity leadership.

Leveraging an established customer-facing service, like Apple Pay or Google Wallet, to which identity can be added as a feature, may be one path to success. Requiring identity verification to cover its incremental cost, rather than the full cost of a new enterprise, changes the economics of the business. The established service can provide a client base to which identity can be added, as well as the trust needed to ask people for personal information. Over time, a base of users and enterprise clients will build. In ZenKey's case, identity was not a sufficient business opportunity for the telcos to market the service themselves, and ZenKey lacked an established customer-facing business to which identity could be added.

Another path is through control of an essential service in a way that only governments can mandate. Presented with the choice of either standing in line at the department of motor vehicles or registering for a government-issued identity wallet to get a driver's licence online, many would register for the wallet. This does not work as well in a competitive market, where suppliers are reluctant to follow this approach in case clients would rather seek more customer-friendly options elsewhere than sign up for the service.

Without either an essential or existing service to leverage, a supplier must be prepared to keep costs low and patiently endure slow, gradual growth before breaking even – which can take years. This type of opportunity rarely excites investors, who are happy to leave the space to tech giants and governments. So far, it's unclear if society is willing to entrust either of those with control of our personal information, even if they were to make the effort.

If it's unlikely that we can guarantee identity online and it's hard to build a business, does our story of digital identity end on a pessimistic note? The internet gave birth to levels of innovation and disruption not seen since the industrial revolution: communication, shopping, commerce, finance, travel, investing and government services have all been revolutionized by going online. There is a continuing explosion of efficiency and prosperity, although some of the benefits are being whittled away by fraudsters. While charlatans seeking to profit from impersonation have been around since long before the internet, opportunities abound for them online, and the likelihood of getting caught is lower than in the real world. Will it always be this way?

While online crime remains a problem, people are growing wiser to the tricks of identity thieves, and measures that add security for new account creation and account access are being put in place. While it still seems unlikely there will be a "magic wand" that puts an end to identity theft, there is gradual adoption of methods and practices to better verify digital transactions. The most promising solution continues to be the addition of "what you have" to "what you know," since stealing a device or SIM card involves more work than copying credentials, is not easy to scale and can't be done from remote global locations. Universal adoption of a device or token that can be presented online would do for digital identity what chip and PIN technology did for retail card payments, forcing fraudsters to look elsewhere for opportunities. Right now, the best candidates for providing such a solution are either the tech companies (such as Google, Microsoft or Apple) or the telcos that manage our mobile devices with unique, secure SIMs – which are often linked to verified identities. The tech companies behind the FIDO Alliance (where FIDO stands for Fast IDentity Online) have created specifications for the "passkey," a cross-company device-based authenticator that may replace passwords. An identity wallet linked to a secure device would also go a long way towards containing identity theft.

Even without a dominant solution, suppliers offering relying parties improved verification tools are making a difference. One such supplier, Onfido, was founded in 2012, in London, England, by three friends who met at Oxford University. It offers document scanning and verification services, as well as online verification by video with liveness detection. According to Onfido, in its most recent year, it prevented US$3.9 billion in fraud losses, enabled online enterprises to reduce fraud rates by 35 percent and helped one enterprise improve secure customer onboarding.[69] After expanding to support more than 1,000 enterprise customers with identity verification, Onfido was acquired in 2024 by Entrust, a global supplier of identity, payment and digital infrastructure solutions.

AuthenticID offers a similar service for scanning and authenticating documents, and ID photo-to-selfie verification. AuthenticID is used by eight of North America's top ten telcos for identity verification when new accounts are created and by their call centres to reduce mobile account takeovers. The software company has developed algorithmic tools and machine learning to detect false documents, synthetic content and deepfake attacks. Stephen Thwaits, AuthenticID's senior vice-president of Global

Solutions, stresses that while their algorithmic solution is not a silver bullet," it is a meaningful innovation in the fight against the evolving methods used by fraudsters.[70]

Trulioo is a private Canadian company with aspirations that go far beyond reduction of identity fraud. Stephen Ufford, Trulioo's CEO from 2011 to 2020, described the company's mission as identity verification for the planet's entire population so that everyone can transact online. He notes that over two billion people are unable to access financial services because they lack traditional identity documentation.[71] The company has established connections to over 450 data partners, with access to information on over five billion people across more than 195 countries. They offer relying parties data matching that verifies personal information against known data sources as well as real-time document analysis and verification.

Onfido, AuthenticID and Trulioo are but three companies. The Identity Management Institute lists fifty-one vendors of identity management services,[72] and the actual number active in this market is far greater. Most relying parties are continuously evaluating new services and layering on those that help contain fraud losses. Over time, these tools will start to reduce the opportunities available to fraudsters, but tools alone will not do the job. Education is also important in containing identity theft, and progress is also being made in this area. Passports, bank cards and, increasingly, our phones are credentials that we rely on to enable activities and transactions; we know to keep them safe, report their loss or theft, and prevent their unauthorized use. Hygiene in the digital world, however, is not as intuitive. We know we should protect the information we use to create online accounts – our name, address, email, phone number and other personally identifiable information – but time and again, we offer them up without much thought. We know we should create strong passwords and turn on multi-factor authentication, but we opt for the convenience of passwords we can remember and shun additional authentication unless compelled to turn it on. The adoption of stronger passwords and multi-factor authentication has been slow, but it is now steadily growing.

Since it's practically impossible to go through life without sharing personal information, we must learn to exercise discretion over the information we share and with whom we share it. Sensitive information, such as that associated with social insurance, licences, bank accounts, payment cards and travel documents, must never be left unprotected, posted on public sites or surrendered unless the requesting party demonstrates a legitimate need. We should be especially careful of any unsolicited request for information by text or email; legitimate enterprises never solicit personal data in that way, directing you instead to their sites or applications when a need arises.

We now take it for granted that our online activities are tracked, our physical location is monitored by the apps on our phones, and financial institutions watch where and when we make transactions. Call centres record conversations, allowing voice biometrics to be used to verify identities of returning callers. If any of this information fell into the wrong hands, it could be used to construct profiles that could assist in identity theft. Fortunately, most of this data is well protected and closely guarded.

Continued progress with digital identity will take time, and big improvements will likely experience false starts. People and enterprises will be suspicious of any party – government or commercial – that tries to position itself as a controlling authority. In the meantime, control will continue to be layered and distributed. The telcos or tech companies that manage our hardware could yet come out with unique, anonymous tokens that link to personal information, which people then manage themselves in keeping with the principles of self-sovereign identity. In this way, the personal device would assume the role that used to be fulfilled by the residential address, with the telco or tech company delivering messages to your phone the way the post office delivered mail to your house or office. Your device would be a proxy for your identity, but you would control your personal information.

This represents a big change, and it will take time to understand how to get there without any negative unintended consequences. We must be careful not to embark on a path that risks making things worse. Fortunately, the identity ecosystem has many checks and balances, and nothing is done quickly. Over time, we may expect that most of the new opportunities the digital world opened up to fraudsters and identity thieves will be closed, but the charlatans and imposters – and the shadow side of human nature – will no doubt remain.

# Conclusion

Herman Webster Mudgett was a man of many talents. In the 1880s, by the time he was twenty-six, he had worked as a teacher, graduated from medical school at the University of Michigan at Ann Arbor, been principal of a grade school and held jobs at a drugstore in Philadelphia and an asylum in Norristown, Pennsylvania. He had also been married, abandoned his wife, defrauded a book publisher and devised a life insurance scheme that used medical cadavers to fake the deaths of the insured. When, in 1886, a child died after taking medicine supplied by the drugstore in which he was working, Mudgett quit his job and hopped on a train to Chicago to start a new life. When he got off the train, he registered himself as a druggist with the state licensing commission, presenting himself as Doctor Henry Howard Holmes. Assuming a new identity was that easy.

When drugstore owner Elizabeth Horton, met "Doctor Holmes," she couldn't ask for his birth certificate, driver's licence or passport, as none yet existed. She couldn't easily consult references. She relied only on her ability to judge the character and capabilities of Doctor Holmes. He was hired, become the drugstore's manager and eventually purchased it to use as a base of operations for his other activity – he was a serial killer who confessed to twenty-seven murders.

The full story of H.H. Holmes is told in Erik Larson's book *The Devil in the White City*. I raise it here only to show that assuming an identity in the real world was once as easy as it is on the internet today and similarly exploited by criminals. The introduction of verifiable documents and credentials has made it much harder to assume a new identity in person, but opening an email or social media account can still be done using any name you like. Establishing a bank account or transferring money online takes more effort, but it's still done with phished credentials or stolen financial information sourced on the dark web. What's more, such online activity can be automated and scaled for repeated execution from anywhere in the world, which makes getting caught extremely unlikely.

Security concerns still keep many services from being offered online, such as voting, accessing medical records and signing contracts. Unless we can be sure a person is who they say they are, not only is personal property at risk, but so are our institutions. If voter turnout increased with the introduction of online voting, could we be sure that the additional votes were cast by those entitled to them? Medical services are already targets for fraudsters, with claims being filed for procedures never performed and services requested using stolen identities. Online insurance and telemedicine would be ripe for attack unless individuals could be reliably identified.

The technology to verify identity online exists. Banks, telcos, Apple and a host of verification service suppliers are finding ways to add "what you have" to "what you know" to verify online identity with levels of assurance similar to those realized in person. The remaining challenges are human, not technical. Overcoming them requires alignment on identity verification methods and business models. Without this alignment, enterprises and government bodies will continue with fragmented approaches, which raise the overall cost, slow adoption and continue the confusion that keeps the door open for identity thieves. However, a mandated common solution is unlikely to be accepted by a population already suspicious of the privacy and surveillance practices of governments and large corporations. How, then, are we to emerge from the crisis?

New generations of digital-savvy consumers will be less likely to succumb to fraud attacks and more likely to understand and embrace online security practices. Technology leaders, both large and small, will continue to introduce increasingly effective verification systems. There will no doubt be a period of turmoil, with many different systems competing for both enterprise and customer adoption. The more effective, privacy-respecting and customer-friendly services will share the benefits, emerging as market leaders while others drop out. Once the market consolidates to three or four leading alternatives, customers will get familiar with legitimate verification methods and be better able to spot the fraudsters. Both customers and enterprises will still be able to choose from among a handful of verification alternatives. Ideally, people will manage their personal information themselves, determining if, when and who gets access to it. The parties seeking verification will pay a small fee for verified identities and people may even realize some revenue from enabling verification.

It may take a decade, or longer, but eventually, digital traffic will reach the level of security and integrity we see in the real world, and may even surpass it. Progress will be made through evolution, not revolution.

# Endnotes

1. Chris Nichols, "An Identity Thief Who Took Demi Moore's AmEx on a Shopping Spree Gets Sentenced," *Los Angeles Magazine*, July 14, 2020, https://lamag.com/celebrity/demi-moore-credit-card-identity-theft.

2. Hollywood Entertainment News, "7 Celebrity Identity Thief Victims," October 22, 2022, https://www.hollywood.com/celebrities/7-celebrity-identity-thief-victims-will-smith-oprah-paris-hilton-more-55000582-60231011.

3. Valentin Groebner, "Describing the Person, Reading the Signs in Late Medieval and Renaissance Europe: Identity Papers, Vested Figures and the Limits of Identification, 1400–1600," in *Documenting Individual Identity: The Development of State Practices in the Modern World*, eds. Jane Caplan and John Torpey (Princeton University Press, 2001), 24, Kindle.

4. Groebner, "Describing the Person," 26.

5. Francis Galton, *Finger Prints*, Macmillan, 1892, 1–2, https://galton.org/books/finger-prints/index.htm.

6. "Fingerprints: The First ID," FindLaw, September 13, 2023, https://www.findlaw.com/criminal/criminal-procedure/fingerprints-the-first-id.html.

7. Groebner, 17.

8. Groebner, 18.

9. Susan J. Pearson, "'Age Ought to Be a Fact': The Campaign Against Child Labor and the Rise of the Birth Certificate," *Journal of American History* 101, no. 4 (2015): 1149.

10. Pearson, "Age," 1145.

11. Pearson, 1165.

12. David Serlin and Valentin Groebner, "Ready for Inspection: An Interview with Valentin Groebner – The Early History of Identity Documents," *Cabinet Magazine* 22 (2006), https://www.cabinetmagazine.org/issues/22/serlin_groebner.php.

13. Paulius Masiliauskas, "Most Common Passwords: Latest 2023 Statistics." Cybernews, November 27, 2023, https://cybernews.com/best-password-managers/most-common-passwords.

14. Andrew Shikiar, "What $10M in Daily Thefts Tells Us About Crypto Security," TechCrunch, June 2, 2021, https://techcrunch.com/2021/06/02/what-10m-in-daily-thefts-tells-us-about-crypto-security.

15. Kim Cameron, "The Laws of Identity," Identity blog, May 11, 2005, https://www.identityblog.com/stories/2005/05/13/TheLawsOfIdentity.pdf.

16. Financial Transactions and Reports Analysis Centre of Canada, "Methods to Verify the Identity of Persons and Entities," Government of Canada, June 1, 2021, https://fintrac-canafe.canada.ca/guidance-directives/client-clientele/Guide11/11-eng.

17. Patricia Meredith and James L. Darroch, *Stumbling Giants: Transforming Canada's Banks for the Information Age* (University of Toronto Press, 2017), 152.

18. Erika McCallister, Tim Grance and Karen Scarfone, "Guide to Protecting the Confidentiality of Personally Identifiable Information (PII)," NIST, April 2010, https://csrc.nist.gov/pubs/sp/800/122/final.

19. Jack Flynn, "40 Fascinating Mobile App Industry Statistics [2022]: The Success of Mobile Apps in the U.S.," ZIPPIA, October 19, 2022, https://www.zippia.com/advice/mobile-app-industry-statistics.

20. Nojoud Al Mallees, "Tim Hortons App Tracked Too Much Personal Information Without Adequate Consent, Investigation Finds," CBC, June 1, 2022, https://www.cbc.ca/news/business/tim-hortons-app-report-1.6473584.

21. Joseph Turow, *Americans and Online Privacy: The System is Broken*, Annenberg Public Policy Center, June 2003, 5, https://repository.upenn.edu/asc_papers/526.

22. Dee Patel, "The Dangers of Sharing Personal Information on Social Media," Penn Today, May 19, 2020, https://penntoday.upenn.edu/news/dangers-sharing-personal-information-social-media.

23. Susan Athey, Christian Catalini and Catherine Tucker, "The Digital Privacy Paradox: Small Money, Small Costs, Small Talk," Working Paper 23488, National Bureau of Economic Research, June 2017, 18.

24. Lana Swartz, "Gendered Transactions: Identity and Payment at Midcentury," *Women's Studies Quarterly* 42, no. 1 and 2 (2014): 137, https://www.jstor.org/stable/24364916.

25. Diners Club International, "The Story Behind the Card," accessed 2023, https://www.dinersclubcanada.com/home/about/dinersclub/story.

26. Swartz, "Identity and Payment," 140.

27. Board of Governors of the Federal Reserve System, *Changes in U.S. Payments Fraud from 2012 to 2016: Evidence from the Federal Reserve Payments Study*, Federal Reserve Payments Study, October 2018, 2, https://www.federalreserve.gov/publications/files/changes-in-us-payments-fraud-from-2012-to-2016-20181016.pdf.

28. Economist, "The Device That Ate Everything?" *Technology Quarterly*, March 12, 2005.

29. GSMA, *Access to Mobile Services and Proof of Identity 2021*, April 2021, 3, https://www.gsma.com/solutions-and-impact/connectivity-for-good/mobile-for-development/wp-content/uploads/2021/04/Digital-Identity-Access-to-Mobile-Services-and-Proof-of-Identity-2021_SPREADs.pdf.

30. GSMA, *Access to Mobile Services*,19.

31. Aaron Smith and Monica Anderson, *Social Media Use in 2018*, Pew Research Center, March 1, 2018, https://www.pewresearch.org/internet/2018/03/01/social-media-use-in-2018.

32. Mary Madden, *Public Perceptions of Privacy and Security in the Post-Snowden Era*, Pew Research Center, November 12, 2014, https://www.pewresearch.org/internet/2014/11/12/public-privacy-perceptions.

33. Daniel J. Solove, *Understanding Privacy* (Harvard University Press, 2008), 1.

34. Lawrence Cappello, *None of Your Damn Business: Privacy in the United States from the Gilded Age to the Digital Age* (University of Chicago Press, 2019), 31.

35. Solove, *Understanding Privacy*, 3.

36. Zenith, "Zenith Forecasts 4.5% Growth for 2023 After 7.3% Uplift in 2022, Marking Continued Healthy Growth," December

5, 2022, https://www.zenithmedia.com/zenith-forecasts-4-5-growth-for-2023-after-7-3-uplift-in-2022-marking-continued-healthy-growth.

37. Annie Palmer, "Facebook Removed 3.2 Billion Fake Accounts Between April and September, More than Twice as Many as Last Year," CNBC, November 13, 2019, https://www.cnbc.com/2019/11/13/facebook-removed-3point2-billion-fake-accounts-between-apr-and-sept.html.

38. PYMNTS, "Nearly 4 in 5 Consumers Screen Dating App Matches on Social Media," April 21, 2023, https://www.pymnts.com/connectedeconomy/2023/nearly-4-in-5-consumers-screen-dating-app-matches-on-social-media.

39. Emma Roth, "Meta Fined $276 Million over Facebook Data Leak Involving More than 533 Million Users," Verge, November 28, 2022, https://www.theverge.com/2022/11/28/23481786/meta-fine-facebook-data-leak-ireland-dpc-gdpr.

40. Gary Bruce, "The Prelude to Nationwide Surveillance in East Germany: Stasi Operations and Threat Perceptions, 1945–1953," *Journal of Cold War Studies* 5, no. 2 (2003): 4.

41. Cappello, *None of Your Damn Business*, 127.

42. Bloomberg Wire, "1 Million Facebook Users Are Being Warned They Might Have Been Hacked," *Dallas Morning News*, October 7, 2022, https://www.dallasnews.com/business/technology/2022/10/07/1-million-facebook-users-are-being-warned-they-might-have-been-hacked.

43. Paolo Zialcita, "Facebook Pays $643,000 Fine for Role in Cambridge Analytica Scandal," NPR, October 30, 2019, https://www.npr.org/2019/10/30/774749376/facebook-pays-643-000-fine-for-role-in-cambridge-analytica-scandal.

44. Fergus Hanson, *Preventing Another Australia Card Fail: Unlocking the Potential of Digital Identity*, Australian Strategic Policy Institute, 2018, 6, https://www.aspi.org.au/report/preventing-another-australia-card-fail.

45. Hanson, *Card Fail*, 6.

46. Louis Menand, "Why Do We Care So Much About Privacy?" *New Yorker*, June 11, 2018, https://www.newyorker.com/magazine/2018/06/18/why-do-we-care-so-much-about-privacy.

47. Jon Agar, "Modern Horrors: British Identity and Identity Cards," in *Documenting Individual Identity: The Development of State Practices in the Modern World*, eds. Jane Caplan and John Torpey (Princeton University Press, 2001), 106, Kindle.

48. Agar, "Modern Horrors," quoted from March 12, 1945, *Daily Express*, 110.

49. Agar, quoted from June 26, 1951, court transcript, "Clarence Henry Willcock v. Harold Muckle," 111.

50. June Gibbs Brown, *Birth Certificate Fraud*, Office of Inspector General, Department of Health and Human Services, September 2000, ii.

51. Brown, *Birth Certificate Fraud*, 13.

52. David Shearer, "Elements Near and Alien: Passportization, Policing and Identity in the Stalinist State, 1932–1952," *Journal of Modern History* 76, no. 4 (2004): 836.

53. Cappello, 180.

54. Cappello, 206.

55. Shearer, "Elements Near and Alien," 850.

56. Ann Cavoukian, "International Council on Global Privacy and Security, by Design," *IEEE Potentials* 35, no. 5 (2016): 45.

57. Menand, "Why Do We Care."

58. Alan Beckley, host, "From an Alberta Farm to an Innovative Way for Attorneys to Help Clients Remotely," Inventors Helping Inventors podcast, episode 152, August 2, 2021, https://inventorshelpinginventors.libsyn.com/size/5/?search=152.

59. Concordia University of Edmonton, "A Powerhouse Partnership in Cybersecurity," July 14, 2023, https://concordia.ab.ca/newsroom/newsroom_news/a-powerhouse-partnership-in-cybersecurity/#.

60. John Lancaster, Nicole Brockbank and Farrah Merali, "How Organized Crime Has Mortgaged or Sold at Least 30 GTA Homes Without Owners' Knowledge," CBC, January 23, 2023, https://www.cbc.ca/news/canada/toronto/organized-crime-groups-behind-gta-home-sales-mortgages-without-owners-knowledge-1.6719978.

61. Lancaster et al., "Organized Crime."

62. Treefort Technologies, "Treefort Technologies and the Land Title and Survey Authority of British Columbia (LTSA) Are Working Together to Combat Identity Fraud," January 17, 2024.

63. Moira Daly, Shona McKay and Vivian Smith, "Top 40 Under 40," *ROB Magazine*, April 28, 2000.

64. DIACC Member Consult Hyperion, *The Economic Impact of Digital Identity in Canada. Digital ID and Authentication Council of Canada*, Digital ID and Authentication Council of Canada, 2018, https://diacc.ca/wp-content/uploads/2018/05/Economic-Impact-of-Digital-Identity-DIACC-v2.pdf.

65. Avast, "Avast to Acquire SecureKey Technologies," March 24, 2022, https://press.avast.com/avast-to-acquire-securekey-technologies.

66. United States Patent Number 5,867,802, "Biometrically Secured Control System for Preventing the Unauthorized Use of a Vehicle," February 2, 1999.

67. John 20:24–29 (ESV).

68. Grand View Research, "Identity and Access Management Market Size, Share and Trends Analysis Report by End-use (BFSI, Education), by Component (Directory Service, Provisioning), by Deployment (Cloud, On-premise), and Segment Forecasts, 2023–2030," Report ID: 978-1-68038-564-9.

69. Onfido, 2024, https://onfido.com/company/?utm_source=google&utm_medium=ppc&utm_campaign=BrandU S&gclid=Cj0KCQjwvb-zBhCmARIsAAfUI2uwGt3EItvgPUr-DyOGNKv4f56LrV80fNugt568cJXoAJsOybNYw4CYaAhTLE-ALw_wcB&gad_source=1.

70. Business Wire, "AuthenticID Releases Deep Fake and Generative AI Detection Solution for Businesses," June 11, 2024, https://finance.yahoo.com/news/authenticid-releases-deep-fake-generative-130000062.html.

71. Silicon Review, "Trulioo: Verify Customers Online, Anywhere in Seconds," 2020, https://thesiliconreview.com/magazine/profile/trulioo-verify-customers-online-anywhere-in-seconds.

72. Identity Management Institute, "Identity and Access Management Vendors," https://identitymanagementinstitute.org/identity-and-access-management-vendor-list.

# References

Board of Governors of the Federal Reserve System. *Changes in U.S. Payments Fraud from 2012 to 2016: Evidence from the Federal Reserve Payments Study.* Federal Reserve Payments Study, 2018. https://www.federalreserve.gov/publications/files/changes-in-us-payments-fraud-from-2012-to-2016-20181016.pdf.

Boysen, Andre. "The Need for a National Digital Identity Infrastructure." *Governing Cyberspace During a Crisis in Trust.* Centre for International Governance Innovation, 2019.

Brown, June Gibbs. *Birth Certificate Fraud.* Office of Inspector General. Department of Health and Human Services, September 2000. https://www.govinfo.gov/content/pkg/GOVPUB-HE-PURL-gpo67303/pdf/GOVPUB-HE-PURL-gpo67303.pdf.

Caplan, Jane, and John Torpey, eds. *Documenting Individual Identity: The Development of State Practices in the Modern World.* Princeton University Press, 2001.

Digital ID and Authentication Council of Canada. *PCTF Verified Person Component Overview Final Recommendation V1.0.* Pan-Canadian Trust Framework™ Verified Person, 2020. https://diacc.ca/wp-content/uploads/2020/09/

PCTF-Verified-Person-Component-Overview-Final-Recommendation_V1.0.pdf.

Epstein, Richard A., and Thomas P. Brown. "Cybersecurity in the Payment Card Industry." *University of Chicago Law Review* 75, no. 1 (2008): 203–23.

Federal Bureau of Investigation. *Internet Crime Report 2021.* Internet Crime Complaint Center, 2021. https://www.ic3.gov/Media/PDF/AnnualReport/2021_IC3Report.pdf.

Frankel, Robin Saks. "When Were Credit Cards Invented: The History of Credit Cards." *Forbes,* July 27, 2021. https://www.forbes.com/advisor/credit-cards/history-of-credit-cards.

Franklin, Simon. "Printing and Social Control in Russia 1: Passports." *Russian History* 37, no. 3 (2010): 208–37.

Goodell, Jeff. "How to Fake a Passport." *New York Times Magazine,* February 10, 2002.

Hanson, Fergus. *Preventing Another Australia Card Fail: Unlocking the Potential of Digital Identity.* Australian Strategic Policy Institute, 2018.

Higgins, Lesley, and Marie Christine Leps. "'Passport, Please': Legal, Literary and Critical Fictions of Identity." *College Literature* 25, no. 1 (1998): 94–138.

Lennon, Brian. "The Long History, and Short Future, of the Password." *The Conversation,* May 3, 2017. https://theconversation.com/the-long-history-and-short-future-of-the-password-76690.

Lewis, James A. "Securing Americans' Identities: The Future of the Social Security Number." Statement before the House Ways and Means Subcommittee on Social Security, May

17, 2018. https://www.govinfo.gov/content/pkg/CHRG-115hhrg33871/html/CHRG-115hhrg33871.htm.

Menand, Louis. "Why Do We Care So Much About Privacy?" *New Yorker*, June 11, 2018. https://www.newyorker.com/magazine/2018/06/18/why-do-we-care-so-much-about-privacy.

Meyer, Karl E. "The Curious Life of the Lowly Passport." *World Policy Journal* 26, no. 1 (2009): 71–77.

Neilson, Luke A. *Digital ID, Surveillance and the Value of Privacy – Part One*. Justice Centre Reports and Analysis. Justice Centre for Constitutional Freedoms, April 4, 2023.

Oremus, Will. "Are You Really the Product?" Future Tense, April 27, 2018. https://slate.com/technology/2018/04/are-you-really-facebooks-product-the-history-of-a-dangerous-idea.html.

Pearson, Susan J. "'Age Ought to Be a Fact': The Campaign Against Child Labor and the Rise of the Birth Certificate." *Journal of American History* 101, no. 4 (2015): 1144–65. https://www.jstor.org/stable/44285276.

Serlin, David, and Valentin Groebner. "Ready for Inspection: An Interview with Valentine Groebner – The Early History of Identity Documents." *Cabinet Magazine* 22 (2006). https://www.cabinetmagazine.org/issues/22/serlin_groebner.php.

Shearer, David. "Elements Near and Alien: Passportization, Policing and Identity in the Stalinist State, 1932–1952." *Journal of Modern History* 76, no. 4 (2004): 835–81.

Solove, Daniel J. "'I've Got Nothing to Hide' and Other Misunderstandings of Privacy." GW Law Faculty Publications and Other Works, 2007. https://scholarship.law.gwu.edu/cgi/viewcontent.cgi?article=1159&context=faculty_publications.

Solove, Daniel J. *The Digital Person: Technology and Privacy in the Information Age.* New York University Press, 2004.

Solove, Daniel J. *Understanding Privacy*, Harvard University Press, 2008.

Suk Gersen, Jeannie. "Why the 'Privacy' Wars Rage On." *New Yorker*, June 20, 2022. https://www.newyorker.com/magazine/2022/06/27/why-the-privacy-wars-rage-on-amy-gajda-seek-and-hide-brian-hochman-the-listeners.

Sullivan, Clare. *Digital Identity: An Emergent Legal Concept.* University of Adelaide Press, 2011.

Swartz, Lana. "Gendered Transactions: Identity and Payment at Midcentury." *Women's Studies Quarterly* 42, no. 1 and 2 (2014): 137–53.

Trost, Jennifer. "The Imposter Rule and Identity Theft in America." *Law and History Review* 35, no. 2 (2017): 433–59.

Warren, Samuel D., and Louis D. Brandeis. "The Right to Privacy." *Harvard Law Review* 4, no. 5 (1890): 193–220.